sex Has a Price Tag

Discussions about Sexuality, Spirituality, and Self-respect

sex Has a Price Tag

Discussions about Sexuality, Spirituality, and Self-respect

PAM STENZEL
with Crystal Kirgiss

ZONDERVAN

Sex Has a Price Tag
Copyright © 2003 by Youth Specialties

Youth Specialties Books, 300 S. Pierce St., El Cajon, CA 92020, are published by
Zondervan, 3900 *Sparks Dr. SE, Grand Rapids, Michigan 49546*

This edition: ISBN 978-0-310-74885-4

Edited: Rick Marschall, Lorna M. Hartman, and Linnea Lagerquist
Cover and Interior Design: Jody Langley
Production Assistance: Nicole Davis

Special thanks to Dr. Donald Adema and Dr. Keith Williams, OB/GYN

Printed in the United States of America

15 16 17 18 19 20 /DCI/ 18 17 16 15 14 13 12 11 10 9 8 7 6 5 4 3 2 1

6   **INTRODUCTION**

12   **CHAPTER ONE**
      Things You'll Never Know

20   **CHAPTER TWO**
      I Do, I Don't

28   **CHAPTER THREE**
      There's No Gun Pointed at Your Head

38   **CHAPTER FOUR**
      There's No Such Thing As A Free Lunch

48   **CHAPTER FIVE**
      Physical Consequences—Pregnancy

62   **CHAPTER SIX**
      Physical Consequences—STDs

78   **CHAPTER SEVEN**
      Emotional Consequences—Deep Hurt

90   **CHAPTER EIGHT**
      Spiritual Consequences—Soul Trouble

102   **CHAPTER NINE**
      Choosing a Personal "Financial Advisor"

118   **CHAPTER TEN**
      Some Strategies on Saving for the Future

132   **LETTERS TO PAM**
      Real letters by real kids from real life

142   **BIBLIOGRAPHY**

Whether you're—
a guy, a girl, young, old ...

whether you're from—
a big city, the suburbs, a small town, the country...

whether you've dated—
never, tons, now and then, once or twice...

whether you got this book from—
your parents, your best friend, your boyfriend/girlfriend...

(or maybe you're standing in a bookstore right now, scanning this chapter, trying to decide what you think),

as long as you're a living, breathing human being who is interested in the topic of sex (and that's pretty much everybody, isn't it?) I guarantee that you'll find at least one idea in this book that will affect your life.

But if you're a teenager who is trying to sort through the bombardment of sexual messages you're getting from the media, the schools, your friends, and your parents, not only will I guarantee you'll find at least one idea in this book that will affect your life, I'll go so far as to say that the information contained in this book will change—or even save—your entire life.

Considering the hundreds of books available on dating and sex, that's a pretty bold statement to make. After all, what can one book possibly have to offer that all the others don't?

Have you ever gone shopping for something like shampoo or toothpaste (or any of that other stuff no one wants to spend money on but everyone has to have) and found yourself paralyzed by the ridiculous number of products available?

There are literally hundreds of shampoo options. Different fragrances. Different colors. Different sizes. Different brands. Different features. Different ingredients. Different promises.

Wouldn't it be nice if there weren't so many choices? Or if someone was honest enough to hang up a big sign that said:

ALL OF THESE SHAMPOO PRODUCTS DO BASICALLY THE SAME THING—CLEAN YOUR HAIR. SO QUIT STRESSING OUT ABOUT WHICH IS BEST AND JUST BUY ONE ALREADY!

There are as many different books on sex and dating as there are shampoos. Each one is a little different from the others. There are some great books out there, books that contain truthful information and good advice. You might have read some of them already. There are also some rotten books out there, books full of stupid philosophies and horrible advice. Maybe you've read some of those, too.

Then there are books with information both good and bad. These books might give truthful information but bad advice, or good advice but no truthful information to back it up.

This book is an attempt to offer you both good advice about sex (based on my own personal belief that God is the creator of the entire universe and everything in it, including sex) and solid information to back it up (based on the latest statistics to come out of the medical community).

Why do I think you should have both of these things?

Simple. Because I think God made all of us to be thinking, feeling, and believing creatures. God *always* gives us the freedom to make our own decisions. He *never* attaches us to marionette strings and makes us dance around like a puppet. If that's your idea of God, then you've got him all wrong.

If it's true God lets us make our own decisions, then doesn't it make sense to base those decisions on something concrete? When you're staring at those three hundred bottles of shampoo we talked about earlier, do you ever say to yourself, "Oooh, I think I'll buy this one because it's pink and I *love* pink and besides, the TV commercial says this one is best"?

No. At least I hope not.

You probably choose shampoo based on several things: personal preference (your own belief based on past experience), what your friends have recommended (the wisdom of others), and price (a concrete fact).

Those are good considerations.

Sex and shampoo don't have a lot in common, except for the fact that each one, in its own way, is part of daily life. Sex is obviously much more powerful and important. And yet many of you have probably spent far less time consciously thinking about your sexual attitudes and choices than you have about which shampoo (or toothpaste, or mouthwash, or soap, or zit cream) you're going to buy.

I hope this book will change that.

We'll talk about values and beliefs— what God says about sex. We'll listen to the wisdom of others—what teens and adults have learned through their own experiences, both good and bad.

And then we'll spend a lot of time dealing with solid facts about sex— what is likely to happen if you choose to engage in certain sexual activities in specific circumstances.

By the end of the book, I want you to be able to make wise, well-informed decisions about sex based on your beliefs, the wisdom of others, and concrete facts.

I don't want you to *ever* say, "Ooooh, I really love this one movie where the two people in love decide to have sex before they're married and so maybe someday I'll want to do the same thing even though my folks would freak if they ever found out and even though I know about the whole God-marriage-sex thing so of course I'd be really careful not to do anything stupid like maybe get pregnant which would be so embarrassing so just to be safe maybe I'll only go *almost* all the way and then what's the big deal?"

Listen to me very carefully—

If you have sex outside of marriage, no matter who it's with, no matter how careful you are, *you will pay*. There are consequences. Plain and simple. That's the way it is.

I want you to know what those consequences are so you can make the wisest and safest decision.

Imagine you've just been given a truckload of cash as a gift. After recovering from the shock, you have to make some decisions about what to do with the money. You could spend it all now, save it now and spend it later, or a little of both.

Your sexuality, and specifically your virginity, is like that cash. It's been given to you as a gift. Too many people fail to realize how valuable that gift is, so they don't give serious thought to what they'll do with it. But you have to decide on your own—I can't decide for you, your parents can't decide for you, and your friends can't decide for you—whether you'll save it all, spend it all, or save a little and spend a little.

I happen to believe only one of those three choices is morally right. For those of you who aren't big on morality, I also believe—and this book will tell you why—that only one of those choices is logical and safe.

I've spoken to millions of kids about sex. I also spent nine years counseling young women in a Crisis Pregnancy Center in Minneapolis. One thing I've learned is that *all* teens need the information in this book—including those who go to church, those who go to youth group, even those who call themselves Christians. It's as ridiculous to assume that only non-Christians struggle with sexual behavior as it is to assume that only non-Christians struggle with gossip, lying, jealousy, or any other sin.

Fact: Some non-Christian teens are having sex, some aren't.

Fact: Some Christian teens are having sex, some aren't.

Regardless of whether you have or haven't had sex, and regardless of what you believe or don't believe about God, please read this book.

You may disagree with my opinions. You may disagree with my values. You may disagree with my advice.

But you can't disagree with the facts.

By the way, if you're thinking that this is going to be a book that says, "Sex is bad," "Sex is naughty," or "Anyone who thinks about sex should have their brain hosed out with dish soap," you're wrong.

In fact, the opposite is true. Turn the page and see what I mean…

CHAPTER ONE
Things You'll Never Know

It's the first day of junior high Health class. You're sitting in the back row with your friends. You can't decide if you're excited or nervous. Scared or thrilled. You've been waiting for weeks to learn about important stuff, like s-e-x, but you're not sure you want to be learning it from Mr. Henderson—the seventh-grade basketball coach and personal friend of your parents who also happens to go to your church.

When Mr. Henderson walks into the room, you know things aren't going to be good. He looks mad. No, he actually looks worried. Or maybe scared. He clears his throat, glances at the room, turns to the chalkboard, and starts drawing a diagram. His hand is trembling.

At first the picture looks kind of like a smiley face—two eyes and a little mouth. Then it starts to look like a frog. Make that a smiling frog. *Two* smiling frogs. Wait…make that two smiling frogs doing a strange dance. Without turning around, the teacher says, "Today we'll be discussing the reproductive systems of boys and girls. If anyone giggles, we'll just forget the whole thing and do worksheets for the next six weeks."

He points to the first smiling dancing frog-looking thing and says, "This is the female reproductive system, comprising fallopian tubes, ovaries, uterus and vagina." He points to the second and says, "This is the male reproductive system, comprising urethra, penis, and testicles."

At the mention of testicles, you and your friends start giggling uncontrollably.

The teacher slams down his piece of chalk, shattering it into dust particles, and frantically erases the board. The back of his neck starts turning bright red and his ears quiver nervously. In a stern but shaking voice he says,

"Take out your workbooks, class, and turn to the chapter on personal hygiene. This week we'll study B.O."

So much for that.

Nothing is more likely to kill the thrill of junior high sexual curiosity than the mention of human perspiration.

Sexual curiosity is normal, especially in young children. In their innocence, they realize that a great mystery surrounds the human body and its many functions. In fact,

mystery is exactly the word the Bible uses when describing the relationship between a man and woman.

So how did we end up with the picture of sex so prevalent in today's society?

Let's look at school first. Sex education has managed to reduce the mystery of sex to a simple biological function. "The male penis enters the female vagina. Presto. Sex."

Of course, schools must cover all the bases, so they add the following.

"Sex, by the way, can result in pregnancy or the contraction of an STD, so be sure to use a condom. Let's all open our sample condoms together and practice, um, using them, um, I mean, take a look at them, shall we?"

And then, for good measure, they add one last thing.

"Remember, don't have sex with anyone until you're ready."

With any luck, everyone will pass the class and a whole new population of sexually educated teenagers will hit the halls.

If you missed the unit at school, no problem. Just spend a night in front of the TV.

> **Girl:** "Oh, Jack. We've known each other almost a whole 15 minutes. Don't you think it's time we cemented our love by sleeping together right here, right now?"

> **Jack:** "Yes, yes, yes. And since our time slot is

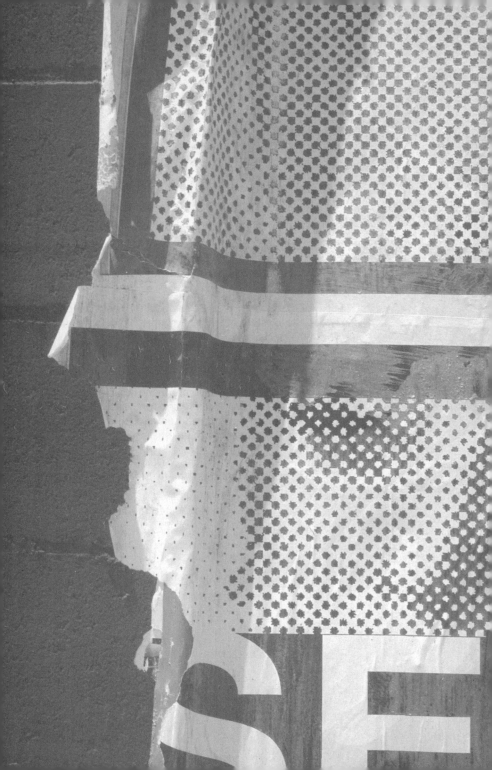

I recently spoke at a high school summer camp held on a prominent Christian university campus. The university nurse was there while I spoke, and when I finished, she asked if I could come back in the fall and speak to the college students. She was really concerned that the information I presented wasn't reaching the college-age group. She told me that lately, she'd had a number of girls come into health services complaining of sore throats. She and her staff had performed strep cultures, but they all came back negative. She'd then suggested to the primary physician that the girls be tested for chlamydia. Sure enough, the tests came back positive.

almost over, there's no time to talk about the pros and cons. Let's just do it, confident that no one will get pregnant, contract a disease, experience any guilt feelings, or regret having slept with such a loser."

Girl: "Thank goodness every sexual encounter is always great and perfect. Who'd want to spoil a sweeps week episode with a disappointing, unfulfilling, and believable act of sex?"

Or maybe you'd rather watch a movie.

Boy: "Hey there, young beautiful lady. Why are you going to jump off the side of this boat into the dark churning waters of the angry ocean?"

Girl: "Because, even though I am beautiful and wealthy, I haven't yet found a dashing young man to sweep me off my feet and have sex with me, thus proving that I am valuable and worthy to walk upon this earth."

Boy: "Hey, if that's all you want, I'm not busy for the next few days. Whaddya say we spend, oh, maybe 48 hours pretending to get acquainted and then get down to business, if you know what I mean. That way, if the boat sinks and one of us drowns, the other one will have great memories for the next 50 years."

Give me a break.

Our society, which claims to know so much about sex, really knows nothing. Actually, less than nothing. If society knew the truth about sex, it would have to remove sex from every TV show, every movie, every book, song, and magazine. Do you know why? Because

sex, the way it was intended to be, could never be reduced to a screen, a CD, or a piece of paper.

Here are some topics that schools and the media will never tell you about sex.

1. Sex is the most awesome, amazing, indescribable, unbelievable, extraordinary tool for giving pleasure to someone you love, but...

2. It promises to be awesome, amazing, indescribable, unbelievable, and extraordinary only in the context of a committed, lifelong, one-man-one-woman relationship (known as marriage), because...

3. In addition to being awesome, amazing, indescribable, unbelievable, and extraordinary, sex is often embarrassing at first and always messy (assuming everything is in good working order), and...

4. Who would willingly risk embarrassment with a person who hasn't proved trustworthy?

5. Why engage in a behavior that is dangerously costly in every instance except one (more on this in chapter 4)?

6. Who'd spend $59.95 on a cheap stereo that will last for only a few months, when you could invest that money for a few years, let the principal and interest grow, and then buy a quality system that will last a lifetime?

Granted, that's a simplified version of things, but you get the idea.

CHAPTER TWO
I Do, I Don't

From the way it's flaunted all over TV, magazines, music, movies, and books, you'd think sex was one of humanity's greatest inventions. The world takes a lot of pride in its sexual knowledge and ingenuity. Society seems to think the biological differences between men and women had no purpose at all until someone got this crazy idea of trying to fit Boy Part A with Girl Part B.

Which makes more sense to you—Adam and Eve accidentally inventing sex after bumping into each other one day in the garden? Or sex being part of the original plan when men and women were created?

In my opinion, it's obvious that sex was part of the original plan—why else would male and female bodies be different, and how else could the human race have survived? In that case, which makes more sense to you—that sex was intended only for reproductive purposes? Or that it had some deeper purpose involving a special relationship of love between two people?

What's more, it's obvious that sex was never intended to be a simple biological function whose sole purpose was to produce more humans. If that were the case, the only reason people would ever have sex would be to create another human being. When's the last time you heard of some guy using this pick-up line:

"Hey, baby, I'm feeling a deep desire to produce another human being,

so whaddya say we have sex even though it's blah, boring, and neither one of us really wants to do it"?

Right.

In fact, creating another human life is the one thing many people *don't* want to do when having sex. Think about it for a minute: what are sexually active teens most afraid of? Pregnancy. Clearly, then, they aren't having sex in order to carry on the human race.

Let's review—

1. Humans did not create sex, God did.

2. Since God created sex, he's the one who understands it the best.

3. Since God understands sex better than anyone, a person who wants to have great sex (and why would anyone want to have rotten sex?) needs to know what God says about sex.

Lucky for us, God isn't keeping the truth about sex a secret. He's one hundred percent willing to give us the inside scoop. Here it is—

Sex was created for one, and only one, situation—marriage. Sex will be all that it can be in one, and only one, situation— marriage.

People who are having sex can be divided into two groups— those who are married and those who aren't. Some people would like to add a few more groups—those who are *almost* married, those who *think they might* get married, those who've *discussed* getting married, etc. Those labels are just an attempt to blur the lines between two clear alternatives, something we're all really good at. If the lines are blurred, it's easier to make excuses for our decisions.

How many times have you had a conversation like this—

Parent: "Did you take out the garbage?"

You: "No, I forgot. I lost track of time. I was busy doing homework. But I *meant* to take it out."

Parent: "Oh, well if you *meant* to take it out, that's good enough for me."

Whatever.

Either you took out the garbage or you didn't.

Either you're married or you're not.

If you are not married, sex is not meant for you.

It's that simple.

Unless my Bible is missing a few pages, I've never read anything about Adam or Eve saying, "Hey God, before committing to this whole man-woman-lifetime-relationship thing, can we have a few weeks to, you know, try things out and see how it goes? I mean, if the sex isn't good, you're going to have to do a little more of your dust magic and create some options for us."

What a nightmare that would have been.

Or how about this scenario—Adam to God: "Hey, thanks for the woman. I'll use her to learn the ropes, you know, get this whole man-woman-sex thing figured out. Then when I'm really experienced, I'll let you know, so you can create someone new and exciting for me."

Please.

Here's another one—Adam to Eve: "I'm interested in hooking up with you now and then. Let's have sex whenever I'm feeling the need. But the rest of the time, I expect you to stay on your side of the garden. And don't be calling me every night just to talk and stuff. I'm not looking for a commitment or anything. If you need to talk, call God."

So much for the sensitive guy.

There are probably a million reasons why God made marriage the dividing line between those who should have sex and those who shouldn't. I'm going to give you two.

First, sex is best in the context of marriage. God's guideline gives you the best.

And second, God's boundary provides the best and protects from the worst.

Clearly, God's way is best. There can be no more blurring of the separating line. It is marriage.

If you haven't said, "I do," you'd better not be doing it.

Guys, sex is not a game. Treating a girl with disrespect is not part of being a man. Because I'm a woman, I can only imagine some of the sexual struggles guys face every day. I don't know firsthand what it's like for you to deal with all that stuff. But I do know this—having sex does not make you a man. Anybody can have sex. It takes no talent or ability. My dog can have sex, for crying out loud.

Having sex doesn't prove you're a man. Having character, integrity, and respect for women is the real proof of being a man.

CHAPTER THREE

There's No Gun Pointed at Your Head

Now that we're all clear on the boundaries for sex—

if you're married, go for it
if you're not, don't

—there shouldn't be any more confusion, right?

Wrong.

The question teens (especially Christian teens) ask me most often is, "If I can't have sex until marriage, then what *can* I do? How far is too far?

Where's the line between having a good time and remaining a virgin?"

In other words, "If I'm not married, how far can I go?!"

Many teens (especially Christian teens) are willing to live within a clear boundary line of "no sex outside of marriage" *as long as* they can create a loophole for certain sexual activity. How is this done? The same way all other loopholes are created—by blurring the lines. In this case, the goal is to make the line dividing "sex" and "not sex" as fuzzy as possible.

I used to think teens were the only ones confused about the definition of sex. But in the past ten years, it's become obvious that a lot of people—even former presidents—are confused about this. Obviously, it's not an age problem.

This might be news to you, but intercourse—the male penis entering the female vagina—is *not* the only behavior that constitutes sex. If you've done a lot of other "stuff" but always stopped short of intercourse, thinking this meant you hadn't had sex and were still a virgin, you may not like what I'm going to say. But I'm going to say it anyway. Why? Because you are too important and too special, and your life is too precious to live without the truth. My job isn't to make you feel good or bad about yourself. It's to give you the truth as clearly as possible.

The medical line that defines sex is this: *Any genital contact at all, whether hand to genital, mouth to genital, or genital to genital, is sex.*

To put it another way,

if you've had any genital contact at all, you've had sex.

These are some of the names for different kinds of genital contact—hand job, oral sex, "outercourse," blow job, etc. You've heard them.

Teens often say to me, "Get real. Oral sex isn't really sex."

There isn't a single married couple who would buy that line. Can you imagine a married man returning from a business trip, informing his wife he'd had oral sex with some stranger, and saying, "But it's no big deal because oral sex isn't really sex."

Or a married woman telling her husband, "You know that guy who works with me and has an office beside mine? Well, sometimes we enjoy touching each other in the genital area, but it's okay because we never get totally naked and we never have intercourse, so it isn't really sex."

So much for being married happily ever after.

If you were married, would you let your spouse get by with that? Would you give your husband or wife permission to mess around with another person as long as they promised not to have intercourse? Of course not.

In the previous chapter, I said that the purpose of sex is not just to reproduce human beings. If it were, then intercourse would be the sole sexual act. Rather, sex is a physical expression of the commitment, trust, and interdependence that defines marriage. That means that sex starts long before a husband and wife are alone in their bedroom. When he puts his arm around her in the morning and says, "I love you," they can be having sex. When she squeezes his hand and smiles at him in a crowd of people, they can be having sex. When two people are married, they can have sex almost anywhere, any time. How great is that?! Who says God doesn't want you to have fun? He wants you to have a *great time*—which is only possible in the right context.

Several years ago, researchers did a study on who was having the best sex. Conventional wisdom says that the people who are having the best sex are those who've had

The ability of sex to bond two people together happens at the conscious and subconscious level. If a guy looks at pornography [or thinks about a girl or imagines being with a girl, etc.] while masturbating, subconsciously he forms a bond with the girl in the picture or his imagination. Over time, this habit creates a "love 'em and leave 'em" condition in the user's sexuality which can make monogamy impossible [or challenging].

a lot of experience with a variety of partners, and who feel free from rules and regulations about sexual activity—in other words, the people who have sex whenever they want with whomever they want.

Guess what?

Conventional wisdom is wrong.

According to the studies,

married Christian women are having the best sex.

That's right. Church women are the most satisfied group of sexually active people. I'm betting their husbands are pretty happy, too.

How cool is that?! Scientific research clearly supports what God's been saying from the very beginning. He's known all along how we can live life to its fullest. If we'd pay more attention to what he says, we'd all be more satisfied and content.

Masturbation is another kind of sexual activity. Essentially, it consists of having sex with yourself. There are many different opinions about masturbation, even within the church. In chapter 8, I'll lay out some of the physical and emotional consequences of masturbation.

Now that you know the medical definition of sex, let me draw a really clear line in the sand. In order to avoid all risks associated with sex and to live within God's boundaries, you must not cross this line: *No genital contact of any kind outside of marriage.*

Or this: *Thou shalt not touch anything that is covered by a modest, grandmother-approved bathing suit.*

Is the line still fuzzy?

If so, read the guidelines again.

Even after seeing the clear medical line in the "what is sex" sand, some of you might still have questions. Instead of asking, "Is everything up to but excluding *intercourse* okay?" now the question is, "Is everything up to but excluding *genital contact* okay?"

These are the kind of people who, if given the big wad of cash we talked about in the first chapter, would be asking, "How much am I allowed to spend?" instead of "How much could I save?" These are the people who are determined to spend at least *something*, just because they can. If that describes you, consider changing your question to this— "How can I save every possible penny *now* so that I can invest it, let it earn interest, and then spend and enjoy it even more *later*?"

Here's a new's flash for you—

waiting for sex has never hurt anyone.

I guarantee.

Guys, you won't die. Nothing will fall off.

Girls, you won't turn into a prude. The world won't cast you aside.

Rather, you will become known as someone who has depth, character, integrity, trustworthiness, and self-control. Someone who isn't controlled by a sexual drive like some animal, who stands for something, who's stronger than hormones, and who respects both yourself and others.

Those things are worth far more than any sexual encounter.

There's a college student I know who's waiting to have sex until he's married. He's the only guy on his football team who's still a virgin. He asked an older man what he could say to his friends when they ridiculed him or mocked his decision. The man said, "Tell them you can become just like them any time you want, but they can never again be like you. That's far more valuable than anything they've ever experienced."

The decision to have sex is exactly that—a decision.

It's a choice. You can say "yes" and you can say "no". You're not a farm animal that can't help itself.

I can't begin to count the number of teens who've said to me, "But Pam, I didn't mean to have sex. It just happened."

Sex doesn't "just happen," not even on the farm. I should know—I'm married to a farmer. At any given time there are some 300 hogs who live outside my back door. They spend pretty much their whole lives doing what comes naturally, but even then, sex doesn't "just happen." The big bad daddy hog still has to make his way over to the big bad mama sow and *do* something.

There are even some teens who go so far as to say, "But Pam, it was an accident."

An accident? Are you kidding?

If you were walking down the street, totally naked, and some blind person of the opposite sex, also totally naked, was walking straight towards you and you ran directly into each other at high speed (because you didn't realize the other person was blind and you expected that person to veer off to the left or right at any second but that person didn't and so *kaboom*), *that* would be an accident. But since we've never heard of that actually happening, it's obvious that the whole "accident" thing is an impossibility.

For those of you who are Christians—who've given your life to Jesus Christ and have a personal relationship with him—the Bible leaves absolutely no question about your behavior.

If you've had sex with someone, it didn't just happen. It wasn't an accident. You chose. You need to admit it, own up to it, and call it what it is…sin. Only then can you ask for God's forgiveness and experience his amazing grace. God promises to forgive all sin and to cleanse us from it (1 John 1:9).

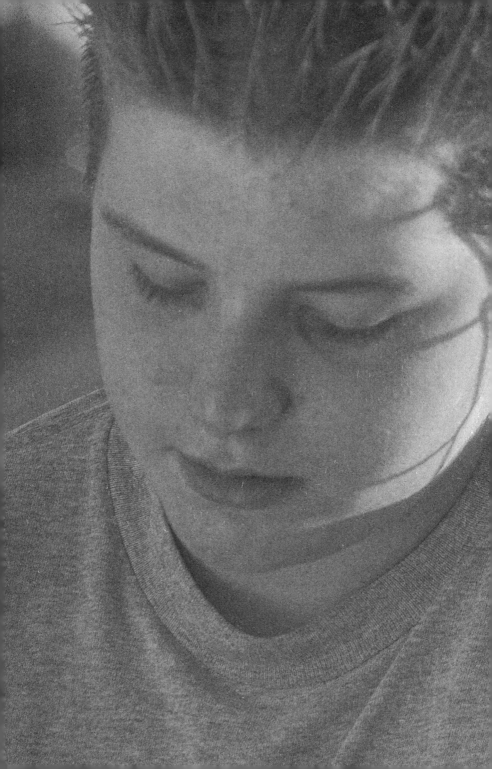

CHAPTER FOUR
There's No Such Thing As A Free Lunch

In case you haven't noticed, we live in a world that loves credit cards.

Practically nobody has enough money to buy everything they want (notice I said want, not need). Even if they did, they probably wouldn't want to spend all the money. Most people want to hang on to their money and have the things they want, so instead of actually buying stuff outright, they charge it.

Some of you have probably gotten offers for your own personal credit card. They seem harmless enough. Buy now, pay later. What could be better than that? In today's world, a person almost *has* to buy on credit. It's expected. It's the norm. It's the way things are. Pay at the pump…with a credit card. Order over the Internet…with a credit card. Purchase through a special TV offer…with a credit card. With a credit card, people get to acquire things without feeling an immediate dent in their pocketbooks. Plus, they don't have to waste precious time earning and saving money ahead of time.

The problem is that nothing is really yours until it's actually paid for, or until it's bought. That means the slogan, "Buy now, pay later," isn't true. It would be more accurate to say,

"Use now, enjoy now, pretend you own it now,

but don't consider it bought until we get our money."

Unfortunately, by the time something's finally paid for, we're often done using and enjoying it.

Here's an example.

Suppose there's a new bike you want (or snowboard, roller blades, guitar, jeans, stereo system, etc.), but you don't have enough money to buy it. Since you really want it, really need it, and really deserve it, you decide to bypass the money issue—you pretend there's no cost—and you charge it. Cool.

Now you've got the new bike (snowboard, roller blades, guitar, jeans, etc.) and you're happy, fulfilled, and content. Plus, it didn't cost you anything.

Yet.

Then the bill comes.

Bad news. You owe $200 (or whatever amount). But good news! You only have to pay $10 a month. That doesn't seem so bad. Of course, your bill is going to have interest added to it each month, so instead of paying $10 a month for 20 months (which, for you math-haters, would equal $200), you're going to pay $10 a month for 25, 26, 27, maybe even 30 months, depending on the interest rate.

By that time, the item you purchased might be broken. You might be tired of it. You might have your eye on the newer model. You might not even like biking (snowboarding, rollerblading, etc.) Too bad. The bill still has to be paid.

There is a cost to everything.

Ignoring the cost does not make it go away.

Millions of people get into financial trouble every year because they continually accumulate things without paying for them up front. They are credit addicts who either don't know how, or aren't willing to calculate the real costs of their purchases.

Guess what? Millions of people get into physical/emotional/spiritual trouble every year for the same reason—because they continually try to accumulate and own things (engage in sexual activity) without paying for them up front (getting married.) They are credit addicts who either don't know how to calculate—or aren't willing to face—the real costs of their actions.

I want to change that. I'm convinced that

if more people knew the real costs of premarital sexual activity,

both immediate and long-term,

they would make different and better choices.

Think of me as a debt counselor or financial advisor for teen sexuality. I'll give you the facts, lay out the truth, and offer a realistic picture of where you'll find yourself in the future based on the decisions you make now.

Most people think of the words "cost" and "price" negatively.

"How much is it going to cost me?"

"That sweater cost you *how much*?!"

"Their prices are way too high."

"I hate paying full price."

People hate paying the price and calculating the cost. It goes against our nature. "Price" and "cost" imply giving up something or doing without something, and neither of those comes naturally. We'd rather *get* than *give up*, and we'd rather have than go without.

We live in a "me first" world.

Check out any TV commercial or magazine ad. I'm positive that you've never seen or read an ad that said, "Our product is pretty great. You should check it out. If it's something that you really need, then you should buy it. If not, well, then why not save your money for something that's really important?"

Right.

Anyway, the point is this—we want, want, want, but we hate to pay, pay, pay.

There are different ways of dealing with this.

You can ignore the cost unintentionally. This happens when you go ahead and fulfill your wants and desires without checking to

see what the price tag says.

When the bill arrives, your response would be surprise. "Bill? For what? You mean I have to pay for that thing?!" Another word for this is ignorance. Usually there's no excuse for igno-

rance except, well, being ignorant.

Or you might ignore the cost intentionally. This happens when you check out the price tag of your want or desire, have a small coronary because the amount is way beyond your budget, and then decide to fulfill your dream anyway, hoping that the bill collector will lose your address. When the bill arrives, you get angry. "Bill? Are you serious? I can't believe you're really going to make me *pay* for that thing!" Another word for this is denial. This is a self-centered and childish act.

Or you might acknowledge and accept the cost. This happens when you check out the price tag of your want or desire, acknowledge that the amount is way beyond what you

can afford, but decide to fulfill your dream anyway, believing the purchase will be worth it in the end. When it comes to teen sexuality, there are two other words for this. In the case of premarital sexual activity, that word is *stupidity.*

The cost is *never* worth the payoff.

In the case of abstinence until marriage, that word is *wisdom.* The cost is *always* worth the payoff.

Yes,

abstinence has a price tag.

If a person decides to pursue a life of abstinence before marriage, there will be a cost. Everything carries a cost. It's your responsibility to *know* the cost, *weigh* the cost, and then decide whether or not the future payoff is *worth* the present cost.

You can play now (the present payoff being sexual activity) and pay later (the future cost is outlined in the next chapters).

Or you can pay now (present cost being abstinence) and play later (and here's the future payoff: a fulfilling sexual relationship in context of marriage).

What does it mean to "pay now" and "play later"?

In the case of abstinence before marriage, the costs of "paying now" might include ridicule (usually delivered by people who need to drag others down in order to feel better about themselves), rejection (usually by a date who views you as a physical object or a sexual conquest instead of as a unique individual), and the frustrating aspects of self-denial (telling yourself "no" even though your emotions or hormones are screaming "yes.")

These are the real costs of abstinence. When Jesus said, "Follow me," "Deny yourself," "Love others," "Don't love the world," he was speaking about every area of life—including sexual activity.

Some people think God is out to spoil all their fun.

They think his laws about sex outside of marriage are nothing more than his way of making life miserable and rotten for human beings.

But God isn't like that at all. I mean, he *did* create sex!

In fact, people willing to pay the price of abstinence will discover that the payoff begins immediately.

Abstinence provides freedom from fear and danger—

the fear of pregnancy, the danger of disease. It provides freedom from emotional pain and guilt. It provides freedom from the pressure to conform to society. It provides freedom from worry about what a future spouse might say or think. It provides freedom from a false evaluation of self-worth. It provides freedom to enjoy life as a teenager without all of the trappings and pressures that go along with sexual activity. It provides freedom to know that someday you'll be able to say to your husband or wife, "Do you know how much I love you? Enough to wait for you…you are the first and only person I will ever know sexually."

Isn't all that freedom well worth the cost of saying "no" to sexual activity and "yes" to abstinence? God's boundaries aren't about messing up your life by denying you the freedom to live however you want. They're about *giving* you the freedom to experience an abundant life, the way God intended it to be lived.

I'll say it again—you have the power to choose between playing now and paying later, or paying now and playing later. The second choice—abstinence—is the wisest and safest—without exception.

The great thing about abstinence is that there are no losers.

I have yet to hear an adult say, "Gosh, I wish I'd had sex with more people before I got married." Or, "Gee, I really regret saving my virginity for one special person." Or, "If I'd just had more sex, more often when I was teenager, I'd probably be a much happier adult."

But I've heard countless adults—and teens—say, "I wish I'd never messed around." "I wish I'd saved myself for my spouse." "I've carried around so much guilt about the past…I wish I'd made different choices."

Here's some financial-sounding advice. It's always better to save your money and pay cash than to put off payments until later. And it's always better to spend the extra money required to get the genuine, top-of-the-line, authentic article.

In sexual terms, that translates into—save yourself sexually for marriage. Be willing to invest yourself in the genuine, top-of-the-line, authentic article. Yes, it means giving up any and all sexual activity right now, but

the return you'll get on your investment will be greater than you could ever imagine.

Ultimately, you're the only one who can decide whether you want to pay or play now. I can't make your decisions for you. Your parents can't make your decisions for you. I can't go on your dates with you. Your parents can't go on your dates with you (even though they probably want to). I can't force you to do or not do certain things. But I can tell you what the consequences and costs are for different decisions.

You know the cost of abstinence. It means paying the price now. And you know the payoff.

The following chapters will tell you about the actual physical costs of engaging in sexual behavior before marriage. The facts are documented. I didn't make any of them up. I won't just be tossing around numbers to convince people that I'm right.

I'm going to tell you the truth because you can handle it. Besides that, the truth will set you free—free to make the best and wisest decision.

CHAPTER FIVE
Physical Consequences—Pregnancy

When I talk to teens about sex, no matter what part of the country I'm in, no matter how big the school or church is, no matter whether I'm talking to girls, guys, or parents, the greatest fear associated with premarital sex is the same.

Pregnancy.

Guys are afraid of getting girls pregnant.

Girls are afraid of getting pregnant.

Parents are afraid of their sons getting a girl pregnant.

Parents are afraid of their daughters getting pregnant.

The fear of "making a baby" haunts everyone.

It used to be that girls were the most fearful. Up until a short while ago, girls carried almost all of the responsibility and dealt with almost all of the consequences. They were the ones who experienced the physical and emotional effects of nine months of pregnancy. They were the ones who were talked about or labeled by their peers. They were the ones who had to contemplate whether or not to quit school or a job. They were the ones who had to go through labor and delivery. They were the ones who…you get the idea.

Recent changes in the law have made guys carry their share of the responsibility. Until the baby is delivered, the guy has no legal rights. The girl can make any decision she wants to regarding the pregnancy. But once the baby is born, things change.

After an unwed mother has given birth, she's required to give the name and social security number of the father. The father will be notified of his child's birth. If he thinks he's not really the father, he has a specific length of time (30 days in many states) to take a paternity test to prove his statement. If he isn't the father, officials will go back to the mother and say, "Sorry. Try again," until they have the real father identified. That's when the real fun begins.

At that point, the father will be held responsible for helping to support that baby financially until the child hits 18. If the father has a job, the state will garnish his wages. If the father gets married several years down the road and begins a family with his wife, he'll still be responsible to support his out-of-wedlock child. Currently,

a teen father will end up paying

a total of between $50,000 and $250,000 (depending on his income) over the next 18 years.

A few years ago, I spoke at a high school in northern Minnesota. When I was done, a popular senior guy stood up and admitted to his classmates for the first time that he was a dad. The summer before, he'd had sex with a girl whose family had been vacationing in the area. They'd had sex once. Neither of them thought they'd see the other one again. They had no plans beyond having a good time one night during summer break.

He worked at a Burger King in town. Money was taken out of each paycheck to help support his baby. That will continue at every job he has for the next 18 years.

Girls, do you want to marry a guy who is already a dad and who will be taking money away from your family in order to support another child?

Guys, what will you say to the girl you want to marry someday if you've already got a child? "By the way, honey, for the next 10 years, a chunk of my take-home pay will be used to provide for my first child, so we're going to have to stick to a tight budget."

How do people try to avoid getting pregnant before marriage? If they're wise enough to deal with the possibility of pregnancy before it actually happens, here's a list of some of the more common "solutions"—

• They use condoms.

• They go on the pill or some other form of birth control.

• They have sex (oral sex, outer sex, mutual masturbation, dry sex, whatever) but not intercourse.

• They have intercourse but stop before the male ejaculates.

• They abstain from sex...*all* sex.

Let's take a look at these five "solutions."

1. Condoms

One out of five condom batches fails to meet U.S. standards.

Not every condom is tested for holes.

Condoms break or slip off 15 percent of the time.

Condoms can be damaged when exposed to extreme heat or cold during transportation.

Condoms are only about 45 percent effective given the way teens use them.

Condoms that are carried around in a pocket or wallet for any length of time are often damaged when the tip (the most vital part) rubs off and wears away because of the guy's normal sitting down/standing up movements.

2. Pill

Side effects include headaches, weight gain, nausea, depression, and more...even blood clots, pulmonary embolism and breast cancer.

A teen girl is 10 times more likely to contract an STD when on the pill because her sense of security regarding pregnancy often translates into having sex with more partners, more often.

The birth control pill is "supposed" to work by stopping ovulation (the egg being completely released by the ovary into the uterus). Because the strength of hormones needed to completely prevent ovulation from occurring is too strong to be safe for women, there is a "back-up plan."

The pill changes the lining of the uterus, making it impossible for a fertilized egg to implant in the wall and thus get the nutrients it needs to grow. Menstruation is induced and this can cause an early abortion.

Many who believe that life begins at conception have moral objections to initiating early abortion by the use of oral contraception.

3. Other sexual activity

It is possible to become pregnant even without having intercourse. Sperm are able to swim up the vaginal canal, through the cervix, and into the uterus whether they are deposited high inside the vagina (as in intercourse) or whether they simply come in contact with the vaginal entrance.

4. Withdrawal

Even before ejaculation, the penis leaks sperm into the vagina, which can result in pregnancy.

One in three females who rely on withdrawal as birth control become pregnant.

5. Abstinence

It is impossible for a girl to become pregnant if she abstains from sexual activity.

It is impossible for a guy to become a father if he abstains from sexual activity. (Gee, what a surprise.)

Here are some sobering statistics—

More than 3,000 teen girls in the U.S. get pregnant every day.

Contrary to popular belief, teen pregnancy is not a minority problem. Seven of 10 teen births in the U.S. are to whites.

Teens can—and many do—get pregnant the first time they have sex.

If a teen couple has sex without birth control, there is a 90 percent chance the girl will get pregnant within one year.

Girls with irregular menstrual cycles have the same chance of getting pregnant as those with regular cycles.

Half the babies born to teen girls 15 to 17 were fathered by men 20 or older.

Nine out of 10 guys abandon their pregnant girlfriends.

Pregnant teen girls are seven times more likely to commit suicide as other girls their age.

One third of teen moms drop out of high school, making it the leading cause of girls quitting high school.

Half of all single young moms live at or below the poverty level. This usually continues *throughout the girl's lifetime.* (On the flip side, if a teen graduates from high school, reaches age twenty, and marries, all before having a child, there is only an 8 percent chance of being poor).

Very few teen moms go on to get a college education.

If a girl finds herself pregnant, there are essentially three options. Not one of them is good.

1. Keeping the baby

She can decide to keep the baby. The statistics above show some of the results of this decision. In addition, most teen moms express feelings of frustration and sorrow about the changes that take place in their lives once the novelty of having a cute, cuddly baby has passed.

They're no longer free to spend time with their friends.

They're totally responsible for another human life 24/7.

They miss out on the activities that are part of teen life.

In short, keeping the baby is rarely the best choice for either the mom or her baby.

2. Abortion

In today's world, both girls and many guys consider

abortion a quick and easy way for a pregnant woman to get out of a sticky situation.

How popular is this "quick fix"? Since 1973, over 30 million abortions have been performed just in America. Teens account for about one-fourth of the abortions performed each year. A third of all teen pregnancies end in abortion.

Consider these facts regarding an unborn child's development from the time of conception—

day 4-8: fertilized egg attaches to womb, sex of baby is determined.

day 19: baby's eyes begin to form.

day 25: baby's heart starts beating.

week 6: baby's brainwaves are detectable, fingers begin developing, nostrils are formed.

week 8: baby's body parts are all present, if not fully developed, including baby's ears, fingers, and toes.

week 8-10: baby begins moving within womb, though mother can't yet feel it.

week 10: baby's heartbeat is strong enough to detect, fingernails are developing, baby can squint, make a fist, swallow, and move the tongue. Brain cells have been, and continue to be, produced at about 250,000 per minute. Everything is in place, needing only fine-tuning.

Where Do I Go for Medical Help?

If you've participated in behavior that puts you at risk for an STD infection, you need to seek medical help. You absolutely must discuss this with your parents. I know what you are going to say: "My parents will kill me!" Though most teens feel that way, there are very few incidents of teens being killed by their parents for seeking STD testing. The truth is, you don't want your parents to be upset at you, to put restrictions on your behavior because you've destroyed their trust, or to be disappointed and hurt. Well, your parents will be disappointed and hurt. You can't dictate their feelings any more than they can dictate yours. You have broken trust as well, and there will be consequences for that. All this is normal and expected. It may not be fun, but again, these are consequences of the choices you made.

You may ask, "Why do I have to tell my parents?" Why? Because they are the people who care the most for you, your future and your life! No matter how much your friends or a youth leader, school counselor, or county health worker may care about you, the reality is that they don't care for you the way your parents do. I cared for any girl who walked through the doors of the crisis pregnancy center—but at the end of the day, I went home to my children, and the day-to-day problems of that young girl were not mine.

Second, you need good medical care, and that requires insurance, payment, and open communication between patient and doctor. Teens typically go to a free clinic because it promises confidentiality. But the free clinic is limited in the tests it is able to offer. The clinic can't follow up on teens' health care, reach them in the future to give them test results, or remind them of follow-up appointments. Basically, their medical care is entirely in their own hands. Most teenagers can't afford the treatment if they do have an STD. Many don't return for follow-up visits, and some never even return to get the test results!

Talk to your parents. Find out who your doctor is and whom your parents trust with your medical care. Make an appointment with this doctor and follow up on your treatment and care. I highly recommend that teenage girls see an obstetrician/gynecologist (OB/GYN), or family practitioners who follow pregnancies and continue care after birth. These doctors specialize in female reproductive treatment and care. They have experience and knowledge in recognizing and treating women's STD infection.

If you chose not to tell your parents, the only option is a free clinic. These are run by county health departments and are listed in the government section of your phone book under Health Services or Health and Human Services. Again, this is not my recommendation. It is in your best interest to include your parents or guardians in your care.

At birth, a baby will have over 100 billion brain cells.

Abortion may appear to be a "solution," but it really isn't.

The procedure is (obviously) fatal for the baby, and risky for the mother. Physically, these risks include—

- Mild to severe infection and/or bleeding

- Damage to internal organs, such as uterus, cervix and urinary tract

- Life-threatening infection due to incomplete abortion (some remaining tissue)

- Scarring, which can lead to infertility

- Pelvic Inflammatory Disease, which can lead to scarring, which can lead to infertility

- among others.

There are also many emotional risks and consequences, such as—

Guilt

Sadness

Heart-wrenching grief

Depression

Thoughts of suicide

Feelings of shame

It is not uncommon for women to carry guilt caused by an abortion with them for the rest of their lives.

3. Adoption

This option is not easy for a pregnant teen. Choosing to give up her baby to another family is difficult. And following through on it can be painful.

But in almost every case, it is the most loving decision she can make for her child. It will provide her child with a loving family. It will provide a husband and wife with a child that they long to love and care for. And it will provide the girl with the reassuring knowledge that she did everything in her power to give her child a solid future.

Almost 40 years ago, a young woman in Michigan found out she was pregnant. To make matters worse, her pregnancy was the result of rape. She was carrying an unplanned child because someone had violated her in the worst way possible.

She had three options—keep the child, have an abortion

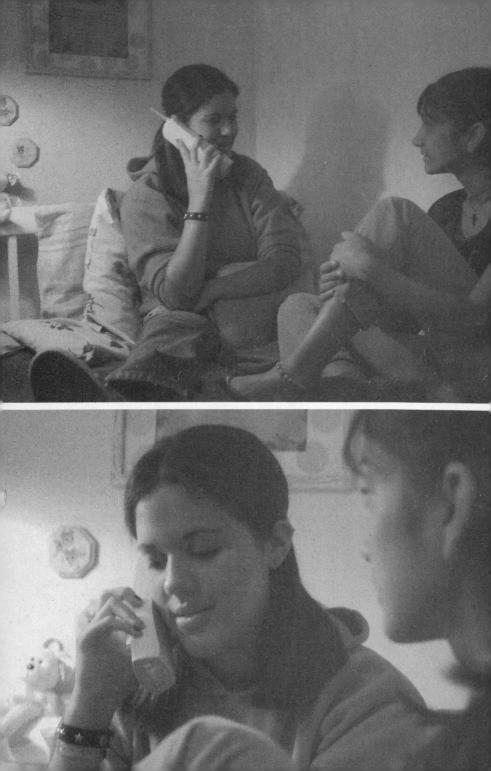

(they weren't legal nationwide, but they still happened), or put the child up for adoption.

Some people might think that in this case, abortion would have been justified.

But this girl did the most wonderful and loving thing she could for the child she was carrying—she placed it up for adoption.

That child was me.

My biological father was a rapist.
I don't even know my nationality.

But I do know this—

just because my father was a rapist doesn't mean I deserved the death penalty.

I've never met my biological mother. But someday I hope to. The first thing I'll say to her is, "Thank you for giving me life. It was the greatest gift you could have given me. And thank you for giving me a loving family, a mother and father to raise me and call me their child. That was the second greatest gift you could have given me."

My biological mom, wherever she is, lived through some very difficult things—being raped, discovering she was pregnant, deciding to let her unborn child have life, and then handing that child over to another person to love and raise.

My biological mom did an amazing thing.

I hope that every teen girl, if she happens to find herself pregnant, thinks carefully about her decision and makes the best choice for her unborn child. The best choice is made much earlier, however—long before this situation could ever arise.

It is the choice to abstain from all sexual activity until marriage. In the context of marriage, even if a pregnancy isn't planned, it is always an amazing, miraculous, and awesome thing that deserves a celebration.

You have the power to decide to live your life in such a way that you'll never have to regret a pregnancy. Instead, you'll always be able to celebrate it.

CHAPTER SIX
Physical Consequences—STDs

Here's a scenario I want you to think about.

A teen girl has sex with her boyfriend—unprotected sex (which includes absolutely everything that happens outside of a monogamous marriage relationship). It's the first time she's ever done anything like this. It was, um, well, it wasn't exactly what she was expecting.

A few weeks later, she misses her period. She's not too worried because sometimes her cycles aren't very regular.

Three weeks later, she still hasn't gotten her period. She thinks about buying a home pregnancy test, but doesn't know where she'd take it. If she does it at home, her mom or dad might find it. None of her friends know what happened, and she doesn't want to tell any of them. Not yet, anyway.

And her boyfriend…well, she hasn't told him that she missed her period. Besides, he's been acting kind of strange and she doesn't feel comfortable talking about this.

So she goes to the local Crisis Pregnancy Center.

She's a little nervous because…well, just because. Because she never thought this could happen to her. Because she can't believe she's here taking a *pregnancy* test of all things. Because being pregnant would totally ruin her life.

A little while later, one of the volunteers comes out and tells her the test is negative.

Negative!

She's so relieved that she can't even speak. It's like someone just lifted a two-ton weight off her shoulders. She feels safe. She feels silly for having been so worried.

She feels free!

She says, "Thanks," flashes the volunteer a huge smile, and heads for the door.

The volunteer says, "Hey, wait a second. You came in here to get tested for pregnancy, right? So why are you leaving? Just because the test is negative? If you were worried about being pregnant,

don't you realize how many other things you should be worried about?

Have you been tested for syphilis, gonorrhea, HPV, chlamydia, herpes, hepatitis A, hepatitis B, trichomoniasis?"

The teen stares at the volunteer in amazement and thinks to herself, *This person has gone off the deep end. Maybe she should consider a career change.*

The volunteer stares at the teen in frustration and thinks to herself, *This person has gone off the deep end. She actually thinks being un-pregnant means her worries are over.*

Listen up—girls, if you get pregnant before you're married, and guys, if you get a girl pregnant before you're married, you've got trouble ahead, that's for sure. But pregnancy might not be your biggest trouble. Why? Because pregnancy is *not a disease*. Newsflash!

Pregnancy is survivable.

Yes, your life will change. Yes, you have some difficult decisions ahead. Yes, you made a big mistake that is going to have a huge effect on your life.

But it's not the worst-case scenario. Really, it's not.

"Oh, right," some of you are thinking, "I forgot about AIDS. Okay, so pregnancy is only the *second* worst thing that could happen."

Wrong.

If you think that pregnancy and AIDS are the biggest dangers involved in sexual activity,

you don't have all the facts. So I'm going to give them to you right now. Don't skip this chapter because you think it doesn't apply to you. This information, in fact, applies to

almost every person reading this book. Guys, it's for you. Girls, it's for you. Guys and girls who haven't had and aren't planning on having sexual intercourse, it's for you, too.

STDs

STD—short for Sexually Transmitted Disease—means just what its name implies: an infection that gets passed from one person to another during sexual activity. From this point on, I'm going to refer to sexual activity as simply sex (remember, that applies to everything that involves genital contact...not just intercourse).

STDs are passed from person to person through body fluids,

secretions, and genital contact. They thrive in warm, moist environments like the human body. The good news (and there isn't much good news concerning STDs) is that STD germs can't survive outside of the human body for very long, so chances are pretty slim that you can get an STD by hugging or shaking hands.

Some STDs are bacterial. This means they can be treated with antibiotics. Unfortunately, many bacterial STDs exhibit few or no obvious symptoms at first, so they go untreated and result in lifelong illness or damage.

Other STDs are viral. This means there is *no cure* for them. Let me repeat—there is no cure. That means if you have one of these diseases, you have it *for life*, and there is a good possibility that you will infect everyone you have sexual contact with after you are infected.

Two generations ago, there were basically two common STDs—syphilis and gonorrhea. Both are bacterial, so they can be treated with penicillin.

Today there are more than 25 STDs.

Here are the facts—

Every year, in the United States alone, more than 12,000,000 people are infected with an STD.

Of those 12,000,000 people, 3,000,000 are teens.

Translated, this means that

one out of every four sexually active teens will contract an STD every year.

Translated a little more, this means that 13 percent of *all teens*—not only the sexually active teens, but *all* teens—will contract an STD every year.

Have you ever heard of Russian Roulette? It's a "game" where one bullet is loaded into a multi-chambered gun. One holds the gun to one's head, pulls the trigger, and hopes to walk away alive.

Compare playing Russian Roulette with a six-shooter to having sex.

You're more likely to contract an STD from sexual contact

than you would be to kill yourself with the gun. If someone said to you, "Hey, how about joining us for a round of Russian Roulette?" I bet you'd say, "Are you crazy!? Not even an idiot would do something that stupid." And yet teens continue to have sex, thinking that if they can avoid pregnancy and AIDS, they'll be fine.

You can get an STD from sexual intercourse. You can get an STD from dry sex/outercourse/mutual masturbation.

And yes, you can get an STD from oral sex.

There are even some STDs that you can get from kissing.

If you don't believe me, read on about teens who thought, "It could never happen to me."

Read the information about each specific STD. You can cross-check all of it with the CDC (the U.S. Centers for Disease Control and Prevention). These are real statistics based on actual test results.

Sometimes I wonder what the numbers would be if *everyone* who had sex was tested...things would be even more grim and depressing.

The good news (and like I said before, there isn't much good news when it comes to STDs) is that STDs are totally preventable.

If you don't engage in any sexual activity until you're married to a person who also hasn't engaged in any sexual activity, you will not be at any risk for these diseases.

That's a guarantee.

If it turned out to be something that didn't require a lot of money or time, wouldn't you immediately grab it?

If there were a way to guarantee you'd never get cancer, wouldn't you want to know what it was?

I'm positive you would. I'm positive *everyone* would.

So then why do so many people choose not to grab the guaranteed prevention for STDs?

Is it because they don't know what it is? Is it because they don't know the truth about STDs?

Is it because they're just too stupid to put two and two together?

I've already told you what the guaranteed prevention is for STDs—sexual abstinence until marriage.

So here's the truth about STDs. Let's take a look at what you might miss out on if you say no to sex.

CHLAMYDIA

This is the most common bacterial infection in the U.S. Teenagers have the highest infection rate of any group. It's estimated that there are 3,000,000 new infections of chlamydia each year. Nearly 85 percent of women and 40 percent of men with this infection report

no symptoms at all.

That's unfortunate, because chlamydia can be treated with antibiotics if diagnosed.

If a female contracts chlamydia just once, there is a 25 percent chance that she will be sterile—unable to have children. If she contracts chlamydia a second time, that number jumps to 50 percent.

A third infection means she has a very good chance of never having children.

Pelvic inflammatory disease (PID) is usually caused by chlamydia. It is painful and results in scarring of the fallopian tubes and uterus.

In addition to infertility—not being able to have children—chlamydia can also cause ectopic pregnancies (the egg implants in the fallopian tube rather than the uterus) and ongoing chronic pain.

Chlamydia can be transmitted during intercourse, oral sex, and any other type of genital contact. People who have never gone "all the way" can, and do, contract chlamydia.

I once counseled a young junior high girl who'd had oral sex with a high school guy. The guy had chlamydia but didn't know it. I told the young girl's mother that she needed to have her daughter tested. "Why? She didn't have sex," was her response. As it turned out, the girl tested positive for the infection.

More than half of all babies born to women with chlamydia will become infected during birth.

HPV (Genital Warts)

Human Papillomavirus (HPV) is the most common viral STD in America. More than a third of all sexually active unmarried people in the U.S. are infected with it. Many don't know it because the symptoms—if there are any—can take months to show up.

There are more than 70 types of HPV. It spreads very easily through simple genital contact. In other words, intercourse isn't required. And

condoms provide little or no protection against HPV.

Think about that...the most common and communicable STD will win the battle against latex almost every time.

There aren't many ways to know if you have HPV. You *might* notice that you have genital warts. I say *might* because (1) some people might not get warts for a long time, if ever, and (2) the warts are often undetected because of where they are located—for example, on the female's cervix. (Have you ever actually seen your cervix, ladies?)

What happens if people get HPV?

First, they will probably give it to everyone they have genital contact with—this includes any skin-to-skin contact of the vagina, vulva, penis, scrotum, or surrounding areas.

Second, they will have to deal with the resulting warts that

In the United States, more than 65 million people are currently living with an incurable sexually transmitted disease (STD). An additional 15 million people become infected with one or more STDs each year, roughly half of whom contract lifelong infections....Yet, STDs are one of the most under-recognized health problems in the country today. Despite the fact that STDs are extremely widespread, have severe and sometimes deadly consequences, and add billions of dollars to the nation's healthcare costs each year, most people in the United States remain unaware of the risks and consequences of all but the most prominent STD—the human immunodeficiency virus or HIV.

While extremely common, STDs are difficult to track. Many people with these infections do not have symptoms and remain undiagnosed. Even diseases that are diagnosed are frequently not reported and counted. These "hidden" epidemics are magnified with each new infection that goes unrecognized and untreated.

From the report "Tracking the Hidden Epidemics: Trends in STDs in the United States 2000", published by the Centers for Disease Control and Prevention (CDC), page 1.

You can read this entire report on the Internet at
http://www.cdc.gov/nchstp/dstd/Stats_Trends/Trends2000.pdf

appear in the genital area. Girls, that includes your vulva and cervix. Guys, that includes your penis and scrotum. These warts must be removed with acid, burning, lasers, or other procedures. However, removing the warts doesn't cure the HPV, which means more warts will continue to develop throughout that person's lifetime. HPV can also cause warts on hands and feet, and recent evidence suggests that parents or adult healthcare workers can pass the disease from warts on their fingers and hands to the genital organs of babies or children that they are taking care of.

Third, they will have to be on the lookout for cancer. HPV is the cause of almost all cases of premenopausal cervical cancer. If a woman's Pap smear shows cancerous or pre-cancerous cells, nine times out of 10 it's because she has HPV. Many people who get cancer resulting from HPV *will never have had any genital warts.*

Don't assume that "no warts" equals "no cancer."

A person who has HPV once has it for life. It can't be cured. Have you seen the television commercial for a new prescription cream that "treats" genital warts? A beautiful woman with long, gorgeous hair rides her mountain bike through the pristine wilderness, then looks into the camera and declares that she won't let genital warts slow her down, no siree. She'll just go buy herself some magical cream that will make her life all better.

Listen up, folks. I don't care how beautiful you are, how athletic you are, or how positive-minded you are. If you have HPV, there's nothing you can do about it except pass it on to others, go through painful appointments to have warts removed, and be diligent about cancer testing.

Trust me. One night of "fun and pleasure" is never, never, never worth the risk.

The only other way to discover HPV is testing: HPV testing is rarely (if ever) done on males. It is very expensive, and most health-care providers deem it unnecessary. This means that boys usually are completely unaware of the infection. A few might have warts on their genital area, but most will not. They will continue to infect their future partners. It amazes me that a boy will actually say to a girl, "I don't have anything; I got tested." Here's what I would ask as a test of my own: "FOR WHAT? And how much did it cost?"

For girls: HPV testing is done by a Pap smear (a test to detect abnormalities in the cells of the cervix). Early discovery and treatment of the precancerous cells on the cervix can prevent them from developing into cervical cancer, which afflicts more than 16,000 women every year, and kills about 5000. Cervical cancer is the second-leading cause of cancer deaths (after breast cancer) in women. At this writing, HPV is responsible for more American women's deaths than is AIDS.

HERPES

Herpes is not a curable disease. Though it isn't especially dangerous (that is, it's not known to cause cancer or infertility), it's painful, embarrassing, annoying, and expensive—and it's terribly infectious. Trouble is, as with many other STDs, people can be carrying the herpes virus and infecting others without knowing it.

Nearly a third of all single, sexually active people contract herpes by the time they're 30 years old. The virus often leads to fever, chills, aches, and painful sores in the genital area and other places. A person with herpes will probably continue having outbreaks of more sores for many years, perhaps even an entire lifetime. These outbreaks are caused by stress, tight clothing that irritates the skin, illness, menstruation, and intercourse.

The greatest danger presented by the herpes virus is to babies.

If a woman's baby is delivered vaginally during her first outbreak of genital herpes, there is almost a one in two chance that the baby will become infected. More than half of infected babies will die. Half of those who survive will be severely brain-damaged.

HEPATITIS B

Three hundred thousand people contract hepatitis in the U.S. each year. Almost one-third of those people will have "silent" hepatitis, with few or no obvious symptoms such as headache, slight fever, aches, fatigue, diarrhea, and nausea. Later, these symptoms can worsen.

Some people who have hepatitis develop a more serious form of the disease and face the risk of liver damage or liver cancer. Some experts estimate that over a million people in the U.S. are carriers of chronic hepatitis.

This disease is transmitted through body fluids, including blood, semen, vaginal fluids, and saliva. Any exchange of body fluids—whether through sexual contact, blood transfusions, or broken skin—can transmit the disease.

There is a vaccination available for Hepatitis B.

There is NO vaccination for Gonorrhea, syphilis, HIV/AIDS, etc.

Here's the bottom line: condoms do not protect you from STDs. Refraining from sexual intercourse does not protect you from STDs. Oral sex and any other form of genital contact can, and will, spread STDs.

A lack of symptoms doesn't mean you're disease-free.

Having any kind of sexual contact, even once, puts your life at risk. Why, why, *why* would you do that to yourself? To someone else?

I can't think of a single reason. Not even a really bad reason.

But then, I'm not you.
And only you can decide how to live your life.

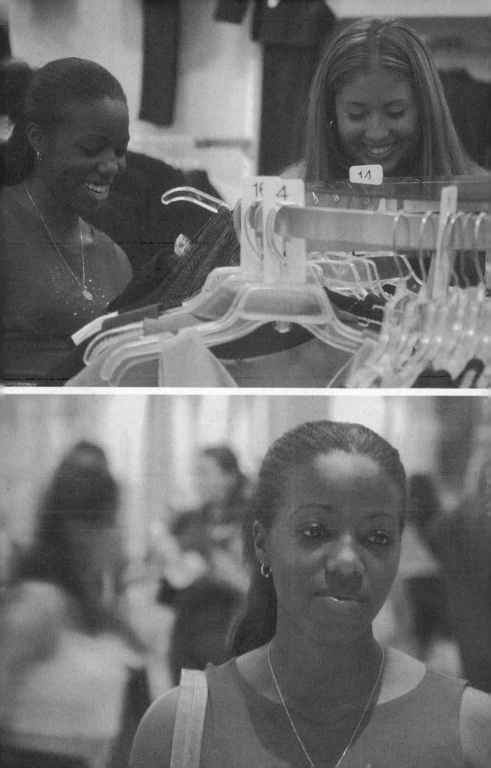

CHAPTER SEVEN
Emotional Consequences—Deep Hurt

If you weren't aware of it before reading this book, I hope the previous two chapters have shown you without a doubt that there are serious physical consequences in store for those who engage in sexual activity outside a monogamous marriage relationship.

Medical facts and statistics can't be denied.

But there are other consequences as well. And though they aren't "proved," "documented," or "diagnosed" in the same way that medical facts are, they're still very real.

I'm talking about emotions.

Emotions are strange things. You can't take a blood test to see if you're suffering from guilt. You can't buy a home kit that tests for depression. You can't visit a clinic to see if you've contracted rejection or mistrust.

Yet guilt, depression, rejection, mistrust, sadness, loneliness, fear, worry, regret, anger, withdrawal, and self-reproach are very real.

Nobody can deny the reality of emotions.

However, people often *do* deny and ignore both the existence and power of emotions in specific circumstances—especially in relationships.

I'll be honest. I can't "prove" the emotional consequences of sex before marriage. All I can do is tell you what the experts say. These experts aren't the doctors, the counselors, or the behavioral scientists. These experts aren't hypothesizing or making predictions based on research or data. These experts aren't even experts in the world's eyes.

Rather, these experts are the people who've personally lived through the emotional aftermath of sex before marriage. They know what they're talking about because they've been there, done that.

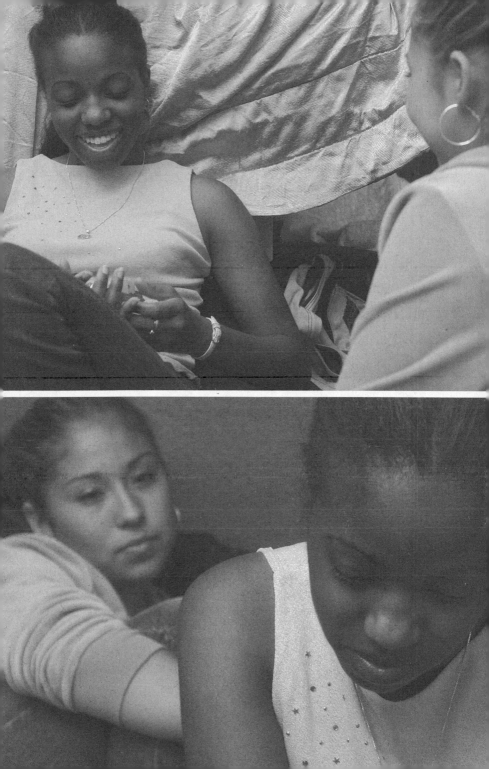

And not a single one of them would choose to have "been there, done that" again if they had the choice.

So, from the experts of all ages and all walks of life, here are the emotional consequences that are in store for those who choose to engage in sex before marriage.

Worry and fear.

No matter how "careful" a couple is, worry and fear almost always accompany sexual activity.

What if someone walks in on us?

What if we get pregnant?

What if my parents find out?

What if the condom breaks?

What if the condom leaks?

What if I can't get the condom on?

What if I don't "do it" right?

What if I don't perform as well as someone else?

What if it hurts?

What if he tells his friends about it?

What if people start to think I'm a slut?

What if ...

But when a married couple has sex—whether it's the first time or the tenth time or the hundredth time—there's nothing to worry about or be afraid of. No one will walk in on you (except maybe your own kids if you've been married long enough to have kids and if you forgot to lock the bedroom door). Your partner won't compare you to anyone else because there won't have *been* anyone else.

If it hurts or doesn't go perfectly the first time after marriage, who cares? Your spouse isn't going to dump you for someone else! You get to work together to create a phenomenal, exciting, satisfying sexual relationship without fear of failure.

No one will consider you a slut, easy, a guy who only wants to get some, or any other derogatory term. When you're married, sex *should* happen, it's *the norm*, it's *expected*, it's *allowed*, it's *encouraged*, and it's *wonderful*—never worrisome or wrapped in fear.

Guilt

Guilt feelings can happen for different reasons. If sex outside of marriage goes against your religious or personal values, you're likely to experience guilt. If premarital sex is something furtive, secretive, and hidden, you're likely to experience guilt (along with fear of being caught).

You're also likely to start viewing sex as something less than beautiful and pure, as something sleazy, because it's happening in a car, on the floor, in a house where other people are present, or some other place where two people can barely grab a few minutes alone. If you're worried about being caught, you begin to associate sex with guilt, and you eventually have a twisted view of what sex is and should be.

Regret

Once a person's decided to have sex, there's no going back and undoing the decision. You can't return it like a pair of jeans that doesn't fit right or a stereo that broke down after only a week. This decision is permanent.

Many regret that they won't be able to give their virginity to their spouse some day.

(Remember, 98 percent of teen couples eventually do get married but not to each other). Many regret going against their own conscience. If an STD is contracted, that's a huge regret, especially since it can often result in lifelong infertility. When the relationship ends, there is regret at having been intimate with and exposing your innermost thoughts and feelings to someone who is no longer part of your life.

Mistrust and loss of respect.

Most couples who have sex outside of marriage report that

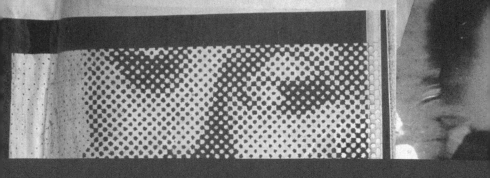

TRUTH AND CONSEQUENCES
Stories of HPV Long-Term Consequences

I could repeat stories like these, over and over again. Some of the details are changed to protect the privacy of those who have shared their personal pain.

I met this young mother at her request for breakfast one morning, and she began sharing a story I've heard all too often. She was a strong Christian and her husband was in ministry. They had met in Bible school when she was 22 and he was 24. He had come to Christ in college and later heard God's call to ministry. Prior to his conversion, he'd had sex with a few girls in high school. He explained this to her, asked her forgiveness, and said his past was behind him. They were in love, so she decided to marry him. Their pre-marriage counseling consisted of discussing how they would handle money and house-hold chores and some theological groundwork on the sanctity of mar-riage. But the past was not discussed. It was the past and was to be forgotten.

Three years after they married, this young woman became pregnant with their first child. About three months into the pregnancy, Ann noticed some growths around her vagina. She went to her doctor, who said she had genital warts that he would simply remove with laser surgery. She had them removed, but the next month, more warts had grown back. She continued to have the warts aggressively treated with a laser every three to four weeks. The laser surgery was painful, and left her vaginal area severely scarred and without feeling. Her doctor had to break the news to her that she had a viral STD for which there was no cure, and that she would simply have to keep getting the warts treated. Ann couldn't understand how her husband could have no warts if he was the one who had given her the virus. As the doc-tor explained it, the virus reacts differently in different people's bod-ies. The hormonal changes during pregnancy probably triggered

the onset and growth of the warts in her. He also explained that in order not to infect her baby with the virus, she would need to have a Caesarean section—she wouldn't be able to deliver the child normally.

Sitting at the breakfast table in tears, Ann shared with me, as her toddler slept next to her, that she was bitter, angry, and unable to be intimate with her husband because of her anger. She said that every time she lay on that table having warts burned off her genital area, she thought of "some girl" who'd given this virus to her husband and she was reminded again that she had not been the only one. As painful as it was, I had to remind her that her husband had not hidden from her his intimacy with other women and that she had forgiven him. Yes, they should've talked about all of the possible consequences... Yes, their pre-marriage counseling should have included a frank discussion of the possible consequences to their marriage of his sexual choices before he came to Christ. However, she chose to marry him knowing his past: her vows said for better for worse, in sickness and in health ... till death do them part. She would have to learn to forgive and heal the relationship for the sake of their marriage and of the little boy who slept by her side. I encouraged her to seek a godly Christian marriage therapist and do the work they should have done long ago.

I never met Ann's husband. I can only guess the pain he must be experiencing as well. He can't go back and change the decisions he made in high school, and I'm sure he had no idea of the consequences that would be paid by his future wife and the damage he would do to their marriage before he even knew her.

When I talk with young men, they usually focus on what the disease means for them. It's very difficult to bring them to realize that the consequences for them may not be life-threatening, but the consequences to their future wives just might be. Young men must think beyond what feels good today in order to protect their ability to feel good for the rest of their lives!

as time goes on, they begin to view one another differently. The girl begins to lose trust in the guy. The guy begins to lose respect for the girl. You might be saying, "That would never happen to us," but that's exactly what these couples thought, too. They were sure they were ready for sex. They were sure they were committed enough and had known the other person long enough. But still, their feelings for one another changed as time went on.

The main regret is probably this—

You have *one chance* to have your first sexual encounter, whether that includes sexual intercourse or something else.

One chance.

Once that one chance has been lost, you'll never get it back again; when you get married, you *won't* be able to say to your spouse, "You are the first person I've been intimate with. You are the *only* person I've been intimate with. I have never become one flesh with another person." But if *you* save that one chance until marriage, you will be able to say it.

If your spouse is also able to say that to you, imagine the trust that you'll have in each other. You'll know that your spouse has self-control, strong values, and the ability to stick with his or her convictions. You'll never deal with mental images of your spouse being with someone other than you. You'll never wonder what the first time was like for your spouse. You'll never think about comparing yourself to a former girlfriend or boyfriend.

You will be free of all those things.

There might be some of you who are thinking, "I totally agree. I would never have sex before marriage...unless I was engaged. Then I might. Since we're going to walk down the aisle eventually, what does it matter? There wouldn't be any emotional consequences in that case."

You're wrong.

First,

God's boundary is *marriage*, not *almost marriage*.

It's simple and clear.

Second, being engaged is no guarantee. People often break off engagements.

Third, the things that happen before marriage affect the things that happen after marriage.

One couple used the term "counterfeit intimacy" to describe the sex they had before marriage. Yes, they eventually got married. Yes, they were both Christians at the time. No, these two facts did not prevent serious emotional consequences that lasted for the first four years of their marriage.

Again, I can't prove these things with charts, graphs, or warnings from the Surgeon General. I can only tell you the true stories of people who've been there.

Is this a risk you're willing to take? Some guys might be thinking, "Emotions might be a problem for girls, but not for me," so you're not going to worry about this issue. Think about this—

somewhere out there is the girl that you're going to marry someday.

Do you want some guy to have sex with her just because he's not worried about his own emotional consequences— let alone hers? If you've ever considered having sex with a girl, remember that she's going to be someone's wife someday. Treat her the way you want your future wife to be treated by other guys. If you don't, you have to face the fact that you lack character and integrity.

I think one of the reasons emotional consequences aren't taken seriously is because there is no prevention for them. People are willing to talk about things like pregnancy and AIDS because they can fall back on the false notion of "protected" or "safe" sex.

"Worried about pregnancy? Don't forget your condom."

"Worried about AIDS? Don't forget your condom."

"Worried about emotional backlash? Um, well, don't forget to ignore your feelings."

There isn't a condom in the world that will protect your heart.

And even if there were, it would completely destroy the purpose of sex, which is to totally give yourself to another person—to a spouse—body, mind and spirit. If you take the emotions out of sex, then you're nothing more than an animal acting out biological urges.

Only human beings can have sex face to face, looking into each other's eyes. Do you suppose that's just by chance?

I don't think so. I think it's because sex, for human beings, involves the soul and heart as well as the body, and eyes are often called "windows to the soul."

Avoid regret, guilt, despair, mistrust, rejection, fear, and all the other possible emotional consequences of having sex before you're married.

Wait.

The cost—paying now—is well worth the payoff—playing later.

CHAPTER EIGHT
Spiritual Consequences—Soul Trouble

I'm from Minnesota.

In Minnesota, fishing is big. Really big. Fishermen take their sport seriously. Very seriously. In Minnesota, it's considered the height of entertainment to get up at the crack of dawn, sit in a shallow boat all day long (regardless of the weather), be perfectly quiet, and impale leeches on the end of a hook that has the potential to get stuck in a person's hand, leg, cheek, eyebrow, or any other piece of exposed skin.

Thrilling, I'm sure.

Did you know that fishing has its own set of rules and strategies? I'm not talking about the legal guidelines (though there are plenty of those, too). I'm talking about the right way and wrong way to fish.

I fish the wrong way.

I possess neither the ability to be quiet for very long, nor the patience to stare at the surface of a lake for hours on end.

If and when I'm actually lucky enough to get a nibble on my hook, I do what any excited fisherwoman would do. I *yank* on the line with everything I've got and start reeling 'er in. This seems logical to me. But it's the wrong way to fish. Consequently, I rarely ever catch an entire fish. However, I have caught more than my fair share of fish lips.

My problem is that I don't play the game very well.

When I feel a nibble, I really should let the line out a little bit. This strategy tricks the fish into thinking that he's not in any trouble, so he keeps nibbling away. It's kind of like a game of cat and mouse, except that there's no cat and no mouse. OK, so it really isn't much like cat and mouse. It's more like, um, a fish and person game.

Let's call it baiting.

Baiting involves all kinds of things—choosing whether to use live bait or a lure, choosing the kind of live bait, choosing the lure, choosing the right water depth, choosing the right strength of line, choosing the right rod, choosing the right lake (or choosing to stay home in bed—my personal favorite).

The key to winning this game is to know your target's weaknesses. If you try to bait a trout using bass strategy, you might as well stay home and read a good book (another personal favorite of mine).

Otherwise, at the end of the day you're going to end up with nothing, or with a big pile of fish lips.

Believe it or not, this is exactly what happens—well, not exactly, but I think you'll get the idea—in the area of sexual activity and temptation.

For the sake of explanation, let's say you're the fish and Satan is the fisherman.

More than anything else, Satan wants to bait and catch you.

He's an expert at this. He knows all about different kinds of fish. He knows all about different kinds of bait. He knows all about water conditions and lake depth. He knows all about baiting, luring, setting the hook, and reeling in the catch.

The first thing he does is pick the right bait or temptation (they're really the same thing). In the case of sex before marriage, his tackle box is filled with a variety of things like media images, "safe sex," birth control, Internet pornography, the *Sports Illustrated* swimsuit issue, locker room jokes, desire for love, suggestive clothing, "everyone is doing it," and a whole lot more.

He tosses the bait out into the water, close enough for the fish to notice, but not so close that his plan is obvious. He wants to tease the fish for a while, get its mind off track, and entice it to check out the bait more closely.

Once he attracts the fish's attention, he waits patiently. The fish checks out the bait. Because the hook isn't obvious, the fish nibbles a little bit. Satan lets the line out, tricking

the fish into thinking he's safe. The fish nibbles a little more. The fish thinks he feels a hook buried inside the bait, so he starts swimming away for safety. Satan lets the line out some more. The fish is able to swim away, and becomes convinced that he isn't really caught, even though something is starting to poke into his gut. The hook embeds itself a little deeper. The fish eats some more of the bait, burps loudly, and notices that his gut is really starting to hurt. Satan lets the line out a tiny bit more. The fish swims farther away, relieved that he hasn't fallen for any stupid bait tricks that everyone is always warning him about. The fish congratulates himself on having escaped any danger.

Satan lets the line out one final time, just for his own amusement, and then *wham!*—starts to reel the fish in…lips and all. He adds the fish to the stringer dangling over the side of the boat in the water. The fish is still alive. But it's caught. It'll never enjoy another leech, worm, or piece of American cheese. And it won't live for long.

James 1:13-18 is a great fishing passage:

When tempted, no one should say, "God is tempting me." For God cannot be tempted by evil, nor does he tempt anyone.

This world is filled with sexually tempting bait. It would be easy to say, "God doesn't really expect me to wait until I'm married before having sex. That may have been the way things worked 2000 years ago, but not now. God says I'm supposed to love others. Well, I love my boyfriend. God created sex. He created love. He created my boyfriend. If he didn't want me to have sex, he wouldn't have made it so hard to say no."

Nice try.

God isn't the one in the fishing boat tossing delectable leeches your way. He's not the one teasing you with the false line of, "Go ahead. It's safe. It'll be worth it. There's no hidden hook."

10 Plus 7 Dangers Of Masturbation

1. Sex happens in the brain first. The arousal response is the most easily trained response in a human being. What we do to prepare the body for sexual response and arousal becomes what we need in order to be aroused. In other words, masturbation trains your body to respond a specific way to specific stimuli.

2. Because of 1, masturbation often becomes addictive.

3. Addictive behaviors are difficult to change.

4. Because of 3, masturbation tends to control the person rather than the person controlling the masturbation. (In other words, it's a habit that's hard to break.)

5. Once the brain has trained a person's sexual response through masturbation or other self-stimulation, the body will continue to require the same activity for sexual response even after a sexual partnership (that is, marriage) has begun.

6. The chemicals released in the brain during sexual stimulation are extremely powerful, and the repeated use of self-stimulation can damage one's ability to respond appropriately to marriage intimacy. (Refer back to 5).

7. It's easier to say no to something before it becomes a habit.

8. Human beings can say no. Masturbation is often encouraged as a way to "deal with sexual feelings and drives that cannot be controlled."

9. Contrary to popular belief, the desire to masturbate does not stop after marriage. It is not a cure for temporarily dealing with sexual pressure before marriage.

10. The most common problems for which married men seek counseling today are pornography and masturbation.

11. The same experts who declare that masturbation isn't addictive go on to claim that guys and girls who masturbate are powerless to stop doing so. So which is it?

12. Saying yes to masturbation (sometimes referred to as "having sex with oneself") in order to say no to having sex with someone else does not make masturbation a good and positive thing. In other words, something that is "less wrong" is not necessarily right. Something that is "less dangerous" is not necessarily safe. And something that is "less false" is not necessarily true.

13. Masturbation takes the mystery of sex and the wonder of "becoming one flesh" with another person and reduces it to something it was never intended to be—a solo activity consisting of a simple biological arousal/release activity rather than something that embraces body, soul, and spirit.

14. Masturbation will not make your hands fall off, your face turn blue, or your brain insane. But that doesn't mean you should do it, does it?

15. Hebrews 13:4 says, "Marriage is to be held in honor among all, and the marriage bed is to be undefiled, for fornicators and adulterers God will judge." The word for fornicators/fornication, pornea, means any sexual behavior, thought, or deed, outside of the sacramental act between a hus-band and wife. Self-stimulation, or masturbation falls into this category. It defiles the marriage bed.

16. Cultivating the self-discipline that's required to say no to masturbation now, before becoming one flesh with a lifelong mate, will develop the strength of character necessary to continue keeping a marriage pure.

17. And one more thing—God forgives freely. Never forget that. At the same time, never use that to justify behavior that goes against God's desire and will for your life.

But each one is tempted when, by his own evil desire, he is dragged away and enticed.

Sexual desire is not a sin. Being physically attracted to someone is not a sin. Sexual urges are not sin.

But *focusing* on sexual desire, physical attraction, or sexual urges—rather than swimming away—will lead to sin.

Then, after desire has conceived, it gives birth to sin;

If you don't swim away when you have the chance, you'll end up taking a nibble of the bait. If you begin to sense there's a hook hidden in there and try to swim away, Satan will play along. He'll give you some line. He'll give you the illusion of being free. "Sure, it's okay. No problem. See, you can get away if you want. You're not in any trouble. Hey, as long as you're not reeled in, you haven't gone too far."

...and sin, when it is full blown, gives birth to death.

Death? Really? Having sex before marriage will lead to death?

If you contract AIDS, yes, but the "death" James is talking about is spiritual. Spiritual death. Separation from God.

People aren't sinners because they sin. They sin because they're sinners.

If a non-Christian has premarital sex, it doesn't make that person a sinner. *Everyone* is a sinner. Our individual sins are simply evidence of that fact.

If a Christian has premarital sex, it doesn't make that person a non-Christian. On the other hand, God doesn't simply say, "Oops, I'll ignore that, just try harder next time." When a Christian sins, his relationship with God needs to be repaired. There's a disconnectedness that needs to be

taken care of.

All that person needs to do is ask forgiveness. 1 John 1:9 says,

If we confess our sins, he is faithful and just and will forgive us our sins and purify us from all unrighteousness.

At that very moment, God wipes that sin away. It's as if it never happened—in spiritual terms. It *doesn't* mean that he wipes away all the physical and emotional consequences. It *does* mean that, when he looks at your heart, that act of sex outside of marriage is nonexistent. That's good news. No...that's great news.

Some people refer to themselves as "recycled virgins." They've engaged in sexual activity before marriage, repented (which means to change direction, not merely say, "Oops, sorry"), and now have a heart that is wiped clean. They'll probably still need to deal with their emotions, and will still need to get tested for STDs...but spiritually, they're clean!

In a marriage relationship, if a husband and wife have an argument, or if one does something that hurts the other, it doesn't make them un-married. They are bound together as one. But the argument, or the hurt, needs to be taken care of. It needs to be cleared up, repaired, forgiven, so the two can be connected again and in a united relationship.

It's the same between God and one of his children, a Christian. When a Christian sins, the bond between that person and God is still there. But the sin needs to be taken care of, cleared up, and admitted so that forgiveness can be received and the relationship can be open again.

One time, a young woman visited me at the Crisis Pregnancy Center where I worked. She was pregnant and afraid of what people would say and what would happen to her life if she had the baby. She looked me in the eye and said, "If I know abortion is wrong, but I decide to get one anyway, will God still forgive me?"

I was silent. What a tough question! I wasn't sure how to answer. Of course God forgives us when we mess up and confess. But what about when we sin intentionally? Romans 6:1 says, *What shall we say, then? Shall we go on sinning so that grace may increase? By no means! We died to sin; how can we live in it any longer?*

In other words, since God promises to forgive us and *wants* to forgive us, should we keep on sinning so he has the chance to forgive us more and more?

Paul's response is, Are you some kind of idiot?! That makes no sense! If God loves you so much, why would you *intentionally* choose to keep on sinning?!

Anyway, my best answer to that young woman's question

was this—my understanding of God is that he will forgive us whenever we go to him and confess. But I also know that he wants, and expects, that we'll grow to the point where we don't take his forgiveness for granted.

That's a long way of saying, God is God and he promises to forgive. But why, why, would you purposely grieve him by deliberately doing something that you know is wrong?

That's a question we need to ask ourselves daily.

One more thing—God is quite clear that he wants our entire devotion.

If you're sexually active, you are not giving God your entire devotion.

You're trying to serve two gods—God and physical pleasure (sex). Romans 8:5 says, *Those who live according to the sinful nature have their minds set on what that nature desires, but those who live in accordance with the Spirit have their minds set on what the Spirit desires.*

1 Kings tells the story of Elijah, a single prophet of God, in a showdown with 450 prophets of Baal. Baal was the god of flocks and fertility. (In farming country, that translates into money, success, and sex.) Many people think Elijah was battling against the prophets of Baal because the people had abandoned God and decided to follow Baal. But in fact, Elijah said to the people, *How long will you waver between two opinions? If the Lord is God, follow him; but if Baal is God, follow him.* (1 Kings 18:21)

God was angry because his people were trying to follow both him and Baal. He wanted their wishy-washiness to end.

So the question for us today is, How long will we waver between two opinions? If the Lord is God, follow him; but if money/success/sex is god, follow it.

You have to make a choice.

You cannot serve both God and physical pleasure.

CHAPTER NINE
Choosing a Personal "Financial Advisor"

Recently, a financial investment firm ran a series of TV ads that went something like this. Some famous retired athlete (let's say a football quarterback) is wallowing in self-pity, boredom, and confusion as he works on his less-than-spectacular golf swing. Another famous retired person (let's say the former quarterback's Super Bowl-winning coach and best friend) enters the scene and shows off his own polished, fantastic golf swing. The depressed retired athlete perks up a bit and says, "Can you help me out here?" The retired coach looks thoughtful for a moment, then says something like, "Hold on to your short-term investments. Diversify your portfolio. Reconsider your long-term ventures. Check out the foreign markets. And, oh yeah, think about taking up badminton."

The narrator closes the scene with this line: "Wouldn't it be nice if the person you trusted the most was your investment counselor?"

In today's sex-saturated world, wouldn't it be nice if the person you trusted most was your personal-sexual-decision counselor?

We've talked about a lot of things in this book—God's original design for sex, society's idea of sex, the mixed messages we all get about sex, the consequences (physical, emotional, and spiritual) of sexual activity outside a monogamous marriage relationship, the costs of choosing a sexually abstinent lifestyle, the decision that everyone must make about whether they will play now and pay later or pay now and play later with sex and its consequences, the false concept of "safe" and "protected" sex, and much more.

There's one last thing I want to ask you—who are you going to choose as your advisor when it comes to making sexual decisions?

Maybe you've never asked yourself that question. Maybe you're thinking to yourself, "What's so important about choosing an advisor?" Or maybe you're thinking, "Sex isn't as issue for me. I'm not even dating anyone right now. So I don't need anyone to advise or counsel me."

YES YOU DO!

Maybe sex isn't an issue for you right now. Maybe you're not dating anyone. Maybe you've never been tempted by sexual desire. But

if you don't consciously decide whose message about sex you're going to follow, you'll have actually made a decision.

You'll have decided you don't care, that it doesn't matter to you, that you believe it's possible to go through life walking down the middle of the road and never be in any danger of being hit or run over.

That's a bad and dangerous decision.

There are lots of people out there talking about sex, sharing their opinions, subtly trying to convince others that their viewpoint is right. The media might never come right out and say, "This is what we think about sex and so should you," but it's implied by the fact that the opposing viewpoint is never presented. The teen magazines might never come right out and say, "Abstinence is okay, but so is sex as long as you're ready and careful," but it's implied by the fact that sex and birth control are regular topics.

Parents. Friends. Television. Church. Your group of girlfriends. Guys in the locker room. Movies. Magazines. Novels. Music. Internet. God.

They all have something to say about sex. They all have

ideas, opinions, and advice. How can you possibly choose between them all?

The truth is, you only have to choose between two different things. That's right. All of those opinions, ideas and advice fall into one of two categories—

THE WORLD

All ideas about sex that are different than God's come from the world. If you decide not to follow God's guidelines for sex, then whether you intend to or not, you've decided to follow the world's guidelines.

Here are some things you should know about the world.

It promotes cheap sex. It strips sex of its ultimate purpose and leaves it with little or no meaning. It teaches that a person can separate body, mind, and emotions. It promotes self-gratification. It does a poor and deceptive job of presenting all the facts about the consequences of sex.

Here's what the Bible says about the world and those who follow it.

1. Following the world's advice has a high cost. Ever heard the phrase "selling your soul to the devil"? People who follow the world "sell their soul to the world."

For whoever wants to save his life will lose it, but whoever loses his life for me will find it. What good will it be for a man if he gains the whole world, yet forfeits his soul? Or what can a man give in exchange for his soul?

—Matthew 16:25-26

2. The world's "enlightened viewpoint" on things like sex is really just the opposite— stupidity.

Don't you know that you yourselves are God's temple and that God's Spirit lives in you? If anyone destroys God's temple, God will destroy him; for God's temple is sacred, and you are that temple. Do not deceive yourselves. If any one of you thinks he is wise by the standards of this age, he should become a fool so that he may become wise. For the wisdom of this world is foolishness in God's sight. As it is written: "He catches the wise in their craftiness"; and again, "The Lord knows that the thoughts of the wise are futile."

—1 Corinthians 3:16-20

3. The world's path is a dead end that leads away from living a fulfilled life.

As for you, you were dead in your transgressions and sins, in which you used to live when you followed the ways of this world and of the ruler of the kingdom of the air, the spirit who is now at work in those who are disobedient.

—Ephesians 2:2

4. The world encourages people to do things that feel good and right at the moment without mentioning that many of

SEX QUIZ
Check your sex smarts with these questions

1. The right time to have sex is when you "feel ready."   TRUE / **FALSE**

The right time to have sex is when you're married.

2. Condoms protect against sexually transmitted diseases.   TRUE / **FALSE**

Condoms can reduce the risk of contracting HIV/AIDS, but do not protect against HPV, genital herpes, chlamydia, and other STDs.

3. HIV is the only STD that kills people.   TRUE / **FALSE**

Other STDs, for example, HPV, which often results in cervical cancer—can lead to death. Also, syphilis, chlamydia, and gonorrhea, if untreated, can lead to death.

4. Pregnancy is the worst consequence of premarital sex.   TRUE / **FALSE**

Pregnancy is not a disease. Pregnancy is survivable. Other consequences, such as contracting an STD, are much worse.

5. If you love someone, you should have sex with him/her to prove your love.   TRUE / **FALSE**

Sex is not proof of love. Outside of marriage, the only thing that sex proves is that you chose not to say "no" to sexual temptation. On the other hand, waiting to have sex until you're married does show your future spouse how much you love him or her.

6. If you don't have sex with your boyfriend/girlfriend, you will lose him/her.   TRUE / **FALSE**

If your boyfriend/girlfriend breaks up with you because you wouldn't have sex, you haven't lost a thing. In fact, you've gained something—freedom from a person who was only interested in you as a sex object, not as an individual.

7. If you don't experiment with sex now, you won't know how to have sex when you get married.   TRUE / **FALSE**

Duh! When it comes right down to it, every virgin who's gotten married has figured out how to have sex. The physical act of intercourse is no big mystery.

8. If you want to marry someone, you should have sex with them beforehand to see if you're sexually compatible.   TRUE / **FALSE**

Wrong again. What does "sexually compatible" mean? All men and women can be sexually compatible. The real question is whether two people are committed, not compatible.

9. Couples who live together before they get married divorce less because they know they're compatible after having "tried each other out" beforehand.   TRUE / **FALSE**

Couples who live together before getting married are more likely to divorce than those who don't.

10. You can only get an STD if you have intercourse.   TRUE / **FALSE**

You can get an STD through intercourse, oral sex, dry sex, even (in rare cases) kissing.

11. Oral sex is "safe sex."   TRUE / **FALSE**

Wrong. Oral sex transmits chlamydia, genital herpes, HPV, and other STDs.

12. Once you get married, you won't face sexual temptation anymore.   TRUE / **FALSE**

Wrong again. Why do you think people have affairs? If you can't be sexually responsible now, what makes you think you'll be sexually responsible after marriage?

13. STDs are curable with medication, and there are drugs you can take to cure herpes and genital warts.   TRUE / **FALSE**

Some STDs (bacterial) can be cured with medication if they're diagnosed in time. Viral STDs, such as herpes, genital warts (HPV) and others can not be cured. Ever.

14. Girls who give a baby up for adoption don't care about the child.   TRUE / **FALSE**

Giving up a baby for adoption is probably the hardest thing a girl will ever do. But she does it because it's in the best interest of the child and because she loves the child more than she loves herself.

15. Abortion is easy, quick, and safe.   TRUE / **FALSE**

No, no, and no. Just talk to anybody who's gone through the procedure.

16. Teen boys who father children can decide whether or not they want to be involved in the child's life.   TRUE / **FALSE**

Teen fathers, if they're really irresponsible, may be able to avoid the daily tasks of child-rearing (diapers, feeding, bathing, etc.) but they cannot avoid the financial responsibility. The government will take child-support money from him until the child is 18 years old.

17. People who believe that sex is only meant for a marriage relationship think that sex is bad, disgusting, and shameful. TRUE / **FALSE**

Most of these people actually think much more highly of sex than other people. They believe sex is amazing, miraculous, mysterious, and awesome.

18. The Pill, Norplant, or Depo-Provera will protect you from STDs. TRUE / **FALSE**

Birth control protects against pregnancy, not STDs.

19. If you contract an STD, you'll know it because you'll feel sick. TRUE / **FALSE**

STDs often go undetected because symptoms are sometimes minor or even absent altogether.

20. Only dirty or very promiscuous people get STDs. TRUE / **FALSE**

Nice people who have sex only one time can, and do, get STDs.

21. Very few people actually have STDs. TRUE / **FALSE**

Many millions of people have STDs. These people go to your school, live in your neighborhoods, pass you by each day…

22. If your boyfriend/girlfriend had an STD, he/she would tell you. TRUE / **FALSE**

First, your boyfriend/girlfriend might have an STD and not even know it. Second, if they did have an STD, do you really think they'd go around telling people?

23. Monogamous sex means having sex with only one person at a time. TRUE / **FALSE**

Monogamous sex means having sex with only one person throughout your entire lifetime.

Written and Directed by

OMING JUNE 4

those things will leave people feeling polluted in the end.

Religion that God our Father accepts as pure and faultless is this: to look after orphans and widows in their distress and to keep oneself from being polluted by the world.

—James 1:27

5. The world's ideas and opinions are not just different than God's—they're completely opposite.

You adulterous people, don't you know that friendship with the world is hatred toward God? Anyone who chooses to be a friend of the world becomes an enemy of God.

—James 4:4

6. The world is full of corruption caused by human sin.

His divine power has given us everything we need for life and godliness through our knowledge of him who called us by his own glory and goodness. Through these he has given us his very great and precious promises, so that through them you may participate in the divine nature and escape the corruption in the world caused by evil desires.

—2 Peter 2:3-4

7. The world encourages people to pursue things that have no lasting value.

Do not love the world or anything in the world. If anyone loves the world, the love of the Father is not in him. For everything in the world—the cravings of sinful man, the lust of his eyes and the boasting of what he has and does— comes not from the Father but from the world. The world and its desires pass away, but the man who does the will of God lives forever.

—1 John 2:15-17

8. The world, by rejecting God, has placed itself under the control of evil.

We know that anyone born of God does not continue to sin; the one who was born of God keeps him safe, and the evil one cannot harm him. We know that we are children of God, and that the whole world is under the control of the evil one. We know also that the Son of God has come and has given us understanding, so that we may know him who

*is true. And we are in him who is true—even in his Son Jesus
Christ. He is the true God and eternal life.*
—1 John 5:18-20

I don't want you to get the wrong idea about the world and
think the above verses mean you should lock yourself in a
closet and never come out. Not at all. Jesus spent time in
the cities, in the country, with all kinds of people, going to
weddings, talking about jobs, discussing life, hanging out
with his friends.

It's not wrong for us to live in the world (where else would
we live?) But it is wrong for us to accept the world's ideas
about the meaning of life and the best way to live.

Why?

Because the world did not create life…God created the
world. And the world promptly screwed itself up big time.

Don't go off the deep end and start thinking that cars are
evil, music is evil, jeans are evil, and Nikes are evil. It's the
message that you've got to beware of. And the world's
message—"me first"—is absolutely, one-hundred percent
wrong.

GOD

If you reject the world as your advisor and counselor about
sex, then your only other option is God. Remember, there
are only two ways to live—God's way and the world's way.
Every philosophy, idea, opinion, and belief fits into one of
those two categories.

Here are some things you should know about God.

He created sex to be wonderful, amazing, and indescrib-
ably powerful. Ephesians 5 describes it as a "profound
mystery." Doesn't that sound more valuable than "something you do with your boyfriend or girlfriend when you feel
like it"?

Because he intended sex to be, among other things, powerful, he created a natural and sensible boundary around
it in order to keep everyone safe. That boundary is marriage. God's boundaries aren't meant to restrict people
and minimize sexual pleasure. They're meant to protect

people and maximize our sexual enjoyment.

For example, fire is a powerful thing. When a fire is contained in a furnace, a stove, or a fireplace, it's a good thing. People don't generally say, "I feel so restricted because I have to keep the fire in the fireplace. My life is practically ruined because I'm not allowed to set fires wherever I want. Everyone's out to spoil my fun."

How dumb is that?!

Fire in the fireplace is good. Fire in the middle of my living room floor is bad. And dangerous.

Fire in the campfire ring is good. Fire in the middle of the forest is bad. And dangerous.

When people play by the rules, stay within the boundaries, and view limitations as protection rather than restriction, life is safer and makes sense. It's true on the highways. It's true on the football field. It's true in line at the grocery store.

And it's true with sex.

One more thing—God is very honest about sex. Unlike the world, he doesn't present only half the truth. He's totally up front about the consequences of following him—it costs your whole life. And unlike the world, he gives something back that is worth much more than the original cost. He gives life, "life to the full" (John 10:10).

Here's what the Bible says about God and those who follow him.

1. He speaks the truth to all who want to hear it.

For this is what the Lord says—he who created the heavens, he is God; he who fashioned and made the earth, he found it; he did not create it to be empty, but formed it to be inhabited—he say; "I am the Lord, and there is no other. I have not spoken in secret, from somewhere in a land of darkness; I have not said to Jacob's descendants, 'Seek me in vain.' I, the Lord, speak the truth; I declare what is right."

—Isaiah 45:18-19

2. He wants us to follow him because he created us and loves us. (The world just wants our money.)

How great is the love the Father has lavished on us, that we should be called children of God! And that is what we are!

—1 John 3:1

Check out the entire book of 1 John.

3. God is available to us all the time, not just when it's convenient.

Where can I go from your Spirit? Where can I flee from your presence? If I go up to the heavens, you are there; if I make my bed in the depths, you are there. If I rise on the wings of the dawn, if I settle on the far side of the sea, even there your hand will guide me, your right hand will hold me fast.

—Psalm 139: 7-10

4. God's truth gives us freedom to have real life. (The world's "truth" makes us addicts— of fashion, pleasure, material wealth, and so many other things that have nothing to do with real life.)

Jesus said, "If you hold to my teaching, you are really my disciples. Then you will know the truth, and the truth will set you free." Jesus replied, "I tell you the truth, everyone who sins is a slave to sin. Now a slave has no permanent place in the family, but a son belongs to it forever. So if the Son sets you free, you will be free indeed.

—John 8:32, 34-36

5. God's freedom isn't just for this life—it's forever. (The world has nothing to offer a dead person.)

But now that you have been set free from sin and have become slaves to God, the benefit you reap leads to holiness, and the result is eternal life. For the wages of sin is death, but the gift of God is eternal life in Christ Jesus our Lord.

—Romans 6:22-23

6. God's truth is simple, sensible, and timeless.

Love others.

You'll reap what you sow
(your decisions have consequences, good or bad).

Gossip is dangerous and hurtful.

Laziness and unwillingness to work will lead to poverty.

Choose your friends carefully.

Acting in anger is unwise and dangerous.

Don't be hypocritical—
your actions and words should agree.

Treat others fairly and kindly.

Pride comes before a fall.

Etc. etc. etc. etc. etc. etc.

7. God invites us to follow him, just as we are, free of charge. (The world tells us to follow it by first changing our looks, styles, etc., and, by the way, it ain't free.)

You see, at just the right time, when we were still powerless, Christ died for the ungodly. Very rarely will anyone die for a righteous man, though for a good man someone might possibly dare to die. But God demonstrates his own love for us in this: *While we were still sinners, Christ died for us.* (Romans 5:6-8)

The world. God.

God. The world.

You need to stack them against each other and ask yourself, "Which makes more sense? Which is true?"

I told you at the very beginning of this book that my goal was to give you the truth about sex and its consequences so you could make an informed decision about how you're going to live your life before you get married.

Because I'm a Christian and believe that God created the entire universe—including people and sex—it's important to me that you see and understand how important he is to this discussion.

If you've considered all the facts and decided that sexual abstinence is the only wise and safe path to follow for right now, I hope you've also decided to follow God's path in all the other areas of your life. Abstinence is his idea. That's why it's the best choice.

If you're a Christian and have decided to follow God, I hope you're applying that to your decisions about sex outside of marriage. Abstinence isn't the wisest choice simply because the physical consequences are so dangerous. It's the wisest choice—the only choice—for people who follow God because it's the way he designed life to be lived.

CHAPTER TEN

Some Strategies on Saving for the Future

I hope that after reading about the consequences of sexual activity outside of marriage—physical, emotional and spiritual—you're convinced that abstinence is the best choice for everyone who isn't married. Some of you were probably already committed to abstinence. Others of you might have been sexually involved in the past, but have now decided that you want to stop engaging in dangerous behavior.

No matter which situation you're in, you need a plan that will help you either to continue or to begin investing in your sex savings account.

Proverbs 22:3 says, *A prudent person foresees the danger ahead and takes precautions; the simpleton goes blindly on and suffers the consequences.* (NLT) In other words, a wise person won't ignore the truth about sexual activity and its consequences. A wise person won't brush off the dangers or say, "Nothing bad could possibly happen to me." A wise person won't assume that having the facts is enough: he or she will take precautions—will have a plan.

The opposite of a wise person is a fool. A fool ignores the truth; a fool doesn't take consequences seriously; a fool always makes excuses for mistakes; a fool never accepts responsibility.

Now that you know the truth about sex and its consequences, there is no excuse for you to make foolish choices.

So you need to take precautions and to formulate a plan for abstinence. That's the wise thing to do.

Your personal plan can be just that—personal. It doesn't have to follow a specific formula. There's not a single verse in the Bible that says, "Thou shalt remain abstinent by eating broccoli every Wednesday, running 2.6 miles every Friday, and working in the church nursery two times a month for the next seven years."

Sorry. It's not that easy (which is lucky for those of you who hate broccoli, hate running, and aren't very good with babies).

I want to give you some basic guidelines to follow, and then offer some practical suggestions. You can use any or all of these, depending on your situation and personality. Some might not apply to you at all; others might be just what you need.

Proverbs 20:18 says, "Plans succeed through good counsel; don't go to war without the advice of others." (NLT) In many ways, you are in a war each day. You fight against the world's messages and society's lies about sex (and other things). Paul wrote, *Be strong in the Lord and in his mighty power. Put on the full armor of God so that you can take your stand against the devil's schemes. For our struggle is not against flesh and blood, but against the rulers, against the authorities, against the powers of this dark world and against the spiritual forces of evil in the heavenly realms.* (Ephesians 6:10-12)

You can read about the armor of God in Ephesians 6:14-18. You'll find these verses very helpful, not just in dealing with sexual temptation, but every other struggle you face in daily life.

SOME BASIC GUIDELINES

1. Protect your heart.

Jeremiah 17:9 says, "The heart is deceitful above all things." That's a pretty strong statement. Most people like to think of themselves as fairly good and decent people, but according to the Bible the hearts of people are naturally self-centered. Becoming a Christian means giving your heart to God so that he can transform it, making it God-centered and other-centered instead of me-centered. That transformed heart must be protected. How?

My child, pay attention to what I say; listen closely to my words. Do not let them out of your sight, keep them within your heart; for they are life to those who find them and health to a man's whole body. Above all else, guard your heart, for it is the wellspring of life. Put away perversity from your mouth; keep corrupt talk far from your lips. Let your eyes look straight ahead, fix your gaze directly before you. Make level paths for your feet and take only ways that are firm. Do not swerve to the right or the left; keep your foot from evil. (Proverbs 4:20-27)

The best way to protect your heart is to keep it closely connected to God. Read what he has to say about life and love. Spend time getting to know him. The more closely connected you are to God, the more you'll trust and believe that his guidelines and plans are the best ones for your life.

Abstinence until marriage is God's plan. If you really believe that, it will be much easier to live it out.

Listen, my son, and be wise, and keep your heart on the right path (Proverbs 23:19); *As water reflects a face, so a man's heart reflects the man.* (Proverbs 27:19)

2. Protect your mind.

Becoming a Christian means giving God your heart, as well as your mind. If the heart is the inner core of a person, then the mind is the control center. The things that you believe in your heart will transfer to your mind and affect the decisions you make. In the same way, if your mind gets distracted, it can affect your heart. The two are closely related.

In Mark 7, Jesus said this to his followers: *It is the thought-life that defiles you. For from within, out of a person's heart, come evil thoughts, sexual immorality, theft, murder, adultery, greed, wickedness, deceit, eagerness for lustful pleasure, envy, slander, pride, and foolishness. All these vile things come from within; they are what defile you and make you unacceptable to God.* (Mark 7:20-23, NLT)

Do you see the relationship between your heart and your mind? The things that you think about affect your heart. If you don't protect your mind and thoughts from impurity, then eventually those impurities will reach your heart.

We live in a very visual world. The things we look at have a huge impact on our thoughts. So do the things we read and listen to. In order to protect your mind, then, you must be careful about what you watch, look at, read, and listen to. If you find your mind or your thoughts wandering into dangerous ground, that's a signal for you.

Turn off the show you're watching on TV.

Walk out of the movie. Close the magazine. Stop reading the book. Change the radio station. Walk away from the conversation.

I was speaking to a middle school audience in rural Ohio a while ago. After the assembly a sixth-grade girl went to the school counselor's office and reported that she'd been taking money to perform oral sex on high school boys on the bus. At the end of the school day, I met with the counselor, the girl, and her mother. I encouraged the mom to take her daughter to a doctor and have her tested. The mother's response was, "It was only oral sex, she'll be fine." I carefully explained the dangers and possible consequences of what had been taking place. The mother wasn't convinced. Three weeks later, I got a call. The mother finally had taken the daughter in to get tested. She tested positive for both herpes and gonorrhea of the throat.

I am totally serious.

Don't use the excuse that it's impossible to live that way. It is challenging and difficult, but not impossible. The Bible says, *No temptation has seized you except what is common to man. And God is faithful; he will not let you be tempted beyond what you can bear. But when you are tempted, he will also provide a way out so that you can stand up under it.* (I Corinthians 10:13) (Look back a few verses and you'll see that sexual immorality was one of the temptations being discussed.)

When tempted, no one should say, "God is tempting me." For God cannot be tempted by evil, nor does he tempt anyone; but each one is tempted when, by his own evil desire, he is dragged away and enticed. Then, after desire has conceived, it gives birth to sin; and sin, when it is full-grown, gives birth to death.

—James 1:13-15

Aha...so the trick is to remove yourself from whatever is affecting your thoughts before your thoughts end up dragging you off in the wrong direction.

Let us behave decently, as in the daytime, not in orgies and drunkenness, not in sexual immorality and debauchery, not in dissension and jealousy. Rather, clothe yourselves with the Lord Jesus Christ, and do not think about how to gratify the desires of the sinful nature.

—Romans 13:13-14

Since the children [human beings] have flesh and blood, he [Jesus] too shared in their humanity so that by his death he might destroy him who holds the power of death—that is, the devil—and free those who all their lives were held in slavery by their fear of death...For this reason he had to be made like his brothers in every way...Because he himself suffered when he was tempted, he is able to help those who are being tempted.

—Hebrews 2:14-18

Jesus never sinned, but Jesus was tempted. During the years that he traveled from city to city, he must have seen and heard things that were far from wholesome and pure. So he knows what it's like to stand firm and stay on the right path even when no one else is.

This means you can talk to him about your own temptations and challenges, and he will understand and help you. It says so right there in the Bible.

It's not enough to protect your mind by keeping the bad things out. You must go one step further by actively filling your mind with the right things. The very next verse in Hebrews explains, *Therefore, holy brothers, who share in the heavenly calling, fix your thoughts on Jesus.* (Hebrews 3:1) *Set your minds on things above, not on earthly things. For you died, and your life is now hidden with Christ in God.* (Colossians 3:2-3)

And the peace of God, which transcends all understanding, will guard your hearts and your minds in Christ Jesus. Finally, brothers, whatever is true, whatever is noble, whatever is right, whatever is pure, whatever is lovely, whatever is admirable—if anything is excellent or praiseworthy—think about such things.

—Philippians 4:7-8

3. Protect your body.

A commitment to abstinence begins in your heart by believing that it's God's plan. Then it moves to your mind by making the decision to act in accordance with your heart. Your mind is also where you carefully weigh all the evidence about the consequences of a sexually non-abstinent lifestyle.

The last step is when your beliefs and your decisions are acted out in your life. You are made up of heart, mind, and body. All three need to be on the same page if you want to live life to its fullest. There's one problem, though, and Jesus stated it very clearly. Then [Jesus] returned to his disciples and found them sleeping. "Could you men not keep watch with me for one hour?" he asked Peter. *"Watch and pray so that you will not fall into temptation. The spirit is willing, but the body is weak."* (Matthew 26:40-41) People whose beliefs, words, and actions line up with one another have character and integrity. They are people who can be trusted and relied upon. People whose beliefs, words and actions don't line up are known as hypocrites. Everyone wants to be the first kind of person (at least I've never met anyone who said, "Man, I really wish I could be just a little more hypocritical").

Some of you might be saying to yourself, "this lady has no idea what she's asking of us!"

"The pressure to have sex today is way too strong to fight. I'll try to keep my heart and mind on track, but my body?! No way! When God made those boundaries, the world wasn't like it is today."

In one sense, you're right.

The world was worse.

In many places, sexual immorality was publicly encouraged and accepted. In fact, moral standards were so low that sexual purity was considered unreasonable. (Check out any study Bible and see what they have to say about worldly culture in New Testament times.)

Even so, Paul wrote, It is God's will that you should be sanctified: that you should avoid sexual immorality; that each of you should learn to control his own body in a way that is holy and honorable, not in passionate lust like the heathen, who do not know God.

—I Thessalonians 4:3-5

He didn't write, "Sexual purity is God's desire for you. But He knows how tough things are what with all those hormones and orgies, so don't sweat it if you can't fight your biological urges. You're only human, after all."

But among you there must not be even a hint of sexual immorality, or of any kind of impurity, or of greed, because these are improper for God's holy people.

—Ephesians 5:3-4

Put to death, therefore, whatever belongs to your earthly nature: sexual immorality, impurity, lust, evil desires and greed, which is idolatry.

—Colossians 3:5

The body is not meant for sexual immorality, but for the Lord, and the Lord for the body.

—I Corinthians 6:13

Flee from sexual immorality. All other sins a man commits are outside his body, but he who sins sexually sins against his own body. Do you not know that your body is a temple of the Holy Spirit, who is in you, whom you have received from God?

—I Corinthians 6:18-19

The acts of the sinful nature are obvious: sexual immorality, impurity and debauchery...

—Galatians 5:19

In the same way, count yourselves dead to sin but alive to God in Christ Jesus. Therefore do not let sin reign in your mortal body so that you obey its evil desires. Do not offer the parts of your body to sin...

—Romans 6:11-13

The voices of physical desire and sexual urges are very strong for some people. The only way to avoid acting out those desires and urges is to let the voice of God and truth have the final word.

SOME PRACTICAL SUGGESTIONS

Everyone who is committed to sexual purity agrees that protecting the heart, the mind, and the body are absolutely necessary. The question is—how?

Each person struggles with different temptations. Person A's weakness might not be a problem at all for Person B. The plan and strategy that you follow will depend on your own areas of weakness. So the first thing you need to do is identify those areas, like we discussed in the section about protecting your mind. Then you need to avoid those situations—even if all your friends are there.

Beyond that, here are some suggestions that will be helpful as you begin thinking about how to actively pursue a life of sexual purity.

1. Write a personal commitment statement regarding sexual purity. List the reasons for your decision. List some action steps. Sign it. Date it. Have your parents sign it (and maybe include their own statement about supporting you in this pursuit). Make copies and give to a few people whom you can trust and who will help hold you accountable.

2. Take part in a sexual purity ceremony with your family. Write you own vows stating your decision and your commitment. Include a promise to your future spouse about your actions. Keep a copy so that someday you can show it to your husband or wife on your wedding day.

3. Check out some of the national abstinence programs (like True Love Waits) to see if they can offer you help and support.

4. Date in groups. Never get into a situation where you are alone with a guy or girl. That's right...never. If you're with other people at all times, you're less likely to do something you'll regret later on.

5. Set clear boundaries in every dating relationship. If the boundary is crossed even one time, call it quits.

6. NEVER DRINK (read Genesis 19:30-38 to see how drinking and sex can affect one another).

7. Never remain in a tempting situation (read II Samuel 11-12 and see how staying in a tempting situation snowballs out of control).

8. When all else fails (you've averted your gaze, you've closed the magazine, you've turned off the TV, you've said no, etc.) RUN! (read Genesis 39 and see how running can be the best choice).

9. Never indulge your fantasies. In other words, don't let your mind imagine and dwell on sexual thoughts (read II Samuel 13 and see what happens when someone lets sexual thoughts go unchecked).

10. Surround yourself with people who share your commitment to sexual purity. This doesn't mean that you can only talk to and associate with people who are virgins. This doesn't mean that you look down on or snub people who don't share your convictions. After all, you live in the world and most of the world doesn't buy into God's agenda. It does mean, however, that you'd better have some friends who will encourage, support, and walk alongside you.

11. Be sure to make God part of your plan. Proverbs 16:3 says, *Commit to the Lord whatever you do, and your plans will succeed*.

Based on what the entire Bible teaches, this means if you will commit to the Lord your plans and desires that are in agreement with His plans and desires, those plans and desires will succeed.

Since it's clear that God's plan is for sex to be contained inside a life-long marriage relationship, then your desire to be sexually pure can happen if you commit it to God and let him guide you.

Proverbs 3:5-6 says, *Trust in the Lord with all your heart and lean not on your own understanding; in all your ways acknowledge him, and he will make your paths straight.* All three parts of you are included in these verses—your heart, your mind (understanding), and the actions of your body (straight paths).

Trust God—believe that his plan is best.

Don't lean on your own understanding—admit that sometimes you don't know the difference between right and wrong (see Proverbs 16:25).

Acknowledge him always—don't exclude him from any areas of your life, especially sex.

That's the best plan you can have. Simple, sensible, and supernatural, all wrapped up into one.

LETTERS TO PAM

Real letters by real kids from real life.

Dear Pam,

I used to go out with this guy, and we broke up after six months. I was hurt for a long, long time. The reason we broke up was because I said I wouldn't have sex with him.

It was three months ago that we broke up, but he came to my house last night and asked me again if I wanted to have sex, and I said no again. He called later and asked me out again that night, and I said I would have to think about it.

I know if I would go out with him again he would still want me to do that, and I know I am not ready. What do you think I should do about this? Thank you for your help.

Anna

Dear Anna,

It sounds like you have already made this decision!

It sounds like you realize that this person really doesn't care about protecting you. It sounds like he wants to have sex, and he keeps hoping you are willing, or that he can wear you down.

I think you are strong enough to not fall for that.

Stay strong,

Pam

Dear Pam,

I have been in a relationship for a year with the same guy, and a couple of months ago we decided to have sex.

Honestly, Pam, I hate it. I hate it because I feel like I am betraying everything that has ever been taught to me by my parents and teachers. In the beginning it seemed so great. I had a special bond with him that no one else had. I felt that was my way of keeping him forever. It is a terrible thing to say, but it's the truth.

I know that people say teenagers can't be in love, but what I feel for him is so strong. It's different from anything I have ever felt. He was also at the assembly today [where you spoke] and this also made him think. When we talked later that day, we both decided that we can't do it anymore. I was the first to bring it up, but he soon agreed with me.

I know that if he really cares about me, then he will wait. My only concern is: Now what do I do?

I want to become a stronger Christian, but I feel like I have messed up so badly already and there is no way I can straighten my life out. This is the only thing that I really am doing wrong in my life. I have always been a good kind of kid. I play softball, swimming, and track. I have a fine relationship with my parents. I have never had any problems with my life until now.

If there is any advice you can give me, I would greatly appreciate it. Should I end the relationship? That isn't what I want, but if it is the only choice, I have to.

Once again, thank you from the bottom of my heart. You are the strongest, bravest person I have met. You are a person of God!

Thank you and God bless.

Hannah

Dear Hannah,

Thank you for your honest e-mail.

I want you to know that you can forgive yourself for this. I think that you and your boyfriend have made a wise decision.

I also don't think that you need to break up, but I would encourage you to be careful. You will want to stay away from situations where you guys may feel tempted to have sex again. You can do this!

Stay strong,

Pam

Dear Pam,

I have been a Christian all my life, and have been to two Acquire the Fire events, and I went to Day One last year, but last night at Acquire the Fire, God used you to talk to me!

You see, when my Mom was 15, like your mom you talked about, she got pregnant with a child and that child was me. As soon as my so-called "father" found out she was pregnant, he left her. I guess she found out what kind of man he was.

He certainly wasn't a man at all, but then my Mom had three choices: 1. She could give me up for adoption. 2. Try and take care of me. 3. She could have an abortion. The fourth, and best choice -- she could have chosen to never have had sex in the first place!

I have always struggled with the feeling that my birth-mom never loved me, I thought, because she gave me away. But last night God showed me that she loved me enough to give me life and put me in a Christian home of blood-bought believers who cared for me!

When you shared your story last night about your mom having you at 15, but then giving you up for adoption, it brought tears to my eyes. My girlfriend and I had been talking about me being adopted...and just then, you were introduced as speaker! And then when you said that about your story, it really touched my heart and I was able to let my birth-mother go, if you know what I mean.

Now I know she loves me, and I am still a virgin because I know the pain it caused, and I will stay that way until I am married!

PJ

Dear PJ,

Thank you for sharing your story with me. You are a special person, and I know that God is going to use you in amazing ways.

Stay strong,

Pam

Dear Pam,

I honestly thought that your speech at our college in Buffalo, NY, would be bull crap, but to tell you the truth, it honestly meant a lot to me. I feel that I have benefited from your speech and I will never forget the importance of waiting until marriage.

It's very hard sometimes to avoid sex. There are so many temptations. As a handsome young man such as myself, I get tempted very often. Oh yeah, before I forget, not only has your presentation allowed me to understand the importance of waiting, but it has also brought me closer to a female that was also at the presentation.

We have known each other for a year now and your speech has motivated us to wait. We have set boundaries for ourselves to better our relationship. I don't know, Pam, but I honestly think that your speech has sparked something very special in my life.

I just want to say that I love you from the bottom of my heart and I hope that you keep on motivating and encouraging young teens such as myself to stay virgins because BEING A VIRGIN IS ABSOLUTELY GREAT!!!

Brian

Dear Brian,

Thank you so much for taking the time to share your thoughts with me. I also congratulate you and your friend for setting boundaries for yourselves. I am proud of you both.

Stay strong,

Pam

Dear Pam,

I was brought up all my life in a Christian home, but like a lot of kids in my position, I felt like my parents were holding me back. They were too strict. My natural response to this of course was to "rebel."

My freshman and sophomore years went downhill. I've never been much of a partier. I would go, but I always thought getting drunk was stupid. Why put yourself and others in that position? Unfortunately, instead I got very dependent on guys and boyfriends.

At the end of my freshman year I lost my virginity. Things kept getting worse with time. I hated going to church, or being with my church friends. Awhile later, I thought I was pregnant. I had every symptom; I would faint, I would get sick every day around 11 o'clock or 1 o'clock and I would feel light-headed and dizzy. And I didn't have my period.

Later, I found out I wasn't pregnant, but my cousin and friends claimed it was a miscarriage. Two days after I found out I wasn't, my boyfriend and I broke up. I was terrified. Two days after that, my own cousin got with him. It hurt so bad to see that.

Anyways, a year later some things in my life got my attention and I decided I needed to get out of my town for the summer and think. I lived with my grandparents for the summer and realized I needed to quit what I was doing. I came home and I had to leave all my old friends and now I'm being home-schooled.

I try to be an example to my friends, but I've also decided not to be around them very much.

Dayna

Dear Dayna,

Congratulations on having the strength to make some changes in your life. I am sure that God will use you to do amazing things.

I think the best advice I can give you is to take it a step at a time. Stay faithful to the small opportunities that God gives you and He will be faithful to give you more opportunities.

Have you been tested for STDs? I think that would be something that you should take care of.

God bless,

Pam

Pam Stenzel
Box 152115
Grand Rapids MI 49515-2115

Dear Pam:

_____
_____
_____
_____
_____
_____
_____
_____
_____
_____
_____
_____
_____
_____
_____
_____
_____
_____
_____
_____
_____
_____
_____

What if I think I might be pregnant?

There are usually Pregnancy Care Centers in your community. They offer free pregnancy testing and will have a counselor there that can help you sort through your feelings and options and give you encouragement throughout your pregnancy, if in fact the test is positive. Once again, they will also encourage you to tell your parents and get them involved, but they usually will be willing to help you do that and be there for you through the process.

You can find the Crisis Pregnancy Center by looking in your yellow pages under "Abortion Alternatives" or "Pregnancy Counseling," or by calling 1-800-395-HELP.

Bibliography

A Return to Modesty: Discovering the Lost Virtue
Wendy Shalit, Touchstone, 1999

Sex: Q and A
National Physicians Center for Family Resources, 2000
www.physicianscenter.org

Boundaries in Dating
Dr. Henry Cloud and Dr. John Townsend
Zondervan, 2000

Why We Stay Together
Ed. Jennifer Schwamm Willis, Marlowe and Company, 2002

The Case for Marriage: Why Married People are Happier, Healthier, and Better Off Financially
Linda J. Waite and Maggie Gallagher, Broadway, 2000

Growing Strong Daughters
Lisa Graham McMinn, Baker Books, 2000

SexSmart: 501 Reasons to Hold Off on Sex
Susan Browning Pogany, Fairview Press, 1998

Sex and Character
Deborah D. Cole, Maureen Gallagher Duran, Haughton Publishing, 1998

Sex: What You Don't Know Can Kill You
Joe S. McIlhaney Jr., M.D., Baker Books, 1997

Notes